# Daughters of Dakota

Volume I:

A Sampler
of stories from the South Dakota Pioneer Daughters
Collection

**Sally Roesch Wagner,** Editor

ISBN 1-880589-01-X (Vol. I)
ISBN 1-880589-00-1 (Set)

- Cover Photo -
With Thanks and Appreciation to:
Dale Claude Lamphere - S.D. Artist
and
The City of Huron, South Dakota
for "The Spirit of Dakota"
Located at the Crossroads Hotel & Convention Center

First Printing 1989
Second Printing 1990
Third Printing 1991
Fourth Printing 1992

DAUGHTERS OF DAKOTA
P.O. Box 349
Yankton, SD 57078

*To*
*Marie Drew*
*who had the vision*
*and the General Federation of Women's Clubs*
*of South Dakota*
*who collected the stories*

## COUNTY MAP FOR THE STATE OF SOUTH DAKOTA

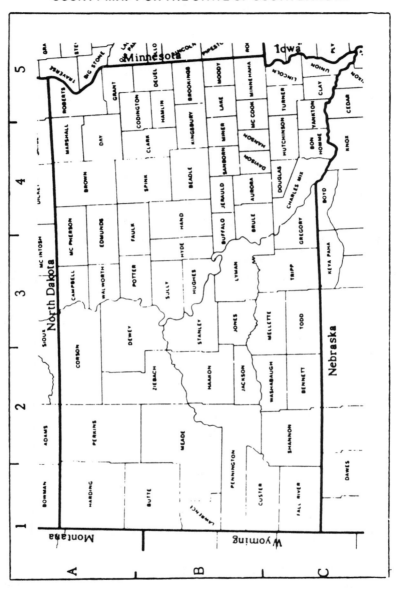

# TABLE OF CONTENTS

vi

# PREFACE

A Pioneer is one who goes before to prepare the way. He [or she] is one who prepares the road for you and me that we may walk more easily in the way and that life itself may be lived more easily and safely. – Marie Drew.

The lilacs were in full blossom in Pierre on that spring afternoon in 1987, and it was hard to keep my mind on suffrage research there in the stuffy basement of the Robinson museum where the South Dakota Historical Society archives were housed. Linda Sommer, the State Archivist, came by and suggested that I take a look at the Pioneer Daughters collection before I leave. When Librarian Associate Bonnie Gardner also suggested that I look at the papers, I decided the lilacs could wait a few minutes while I glanced through the collection.

Five minutes later, my researcher's eye knew that this was a find of a lifetime: a four-drawer file cabinet packed with stories of pioneer women telling honestly, and in their own words, about their experience. Represented was the scope and range of the lives of white women settlers when the land was taken for non-Indian settlement: white and black, rich and poor, native-born and immigrant, representing a spectrum of nationalities, ages, life styles and religions.

How many stories? No one knew for sure, somewhere between 4,000 and 6,000, making this possibly the largest untapped collection of pioneer women's history in the nation. Joanna Stratton's 1981 book, *Pioneer Women,* based on her marvelous discovery of biographical sketches of 800 early Kansas women, was heralded as a first. This South Dakota collection is over *six times* the size of the one Stratton uncovered.

With the state Centennial coming up in 1989, these amazing stories needed to be brought out quickly, made available in some way. Time was running short. A book was an obvious way to do it. But my concern was that the book would come to be identified as *the* Pioneer Daughters, and the thousands of women whose stories were not included in it would be once again relegated to historical invisibility. Two projects seemed possible. One would be to enter a selected representation of the biographies on computer diskettes for use in the schools. The General Federation of Women's Clubs, Office of Equal Opportunity in Education of the Department of Education, State Historical Society and Mary Chilton Foundation of the Daughters of the American Revolution all provided funding and support, and once we had the Daughters of Dakota Curriculum project well underway, (500 stories with an accompanying curriculum unit are now available through the state Department of Education), it was time to begin on the book. One volume extended to at least five, as the stories began to organize themselves into categories.

This is the first volume in the series. It is not a systematic attempt at a representative sample, but rather a sampling of the voices, to give a sense of the rich diversity of these women and their pioneer experiences. Later volumes will look at families and friendship networks of women who homesteaded, the unique experience of women in the Black Hills, diaries and autobiographies, immigrant stories, and longer literary works by these pioneer women. But most importantly, a volume of the surprisingly strong and pervasive history of positive interaction between these pioneer women and the Lakota people who were living on the land, will be brought out in 1990 in time for the centennial of the massacre of Wounded Knee.

If there is a way in which this current volume does not present an accurate sample of the Pioneer Daughters, it is in the sparseness of the numerous stories the collection contains of white women, trained to live in terror of the Indians, and instead finding them friendly, kind and helpful, if a bit culturally incomprehensible. It is these Indian/non-Indian interaction stories that make up, in my opinion, the most important single aspect of the Pioneer Daughters collection.

Following Marie Drew's suggestion that "the English or grammar used is to be the writer's own for history is wanted and not perfect manuscripts," grammatical editing has been done lightly, only for clarity. Since the original stories are available in the South Dakota Historical Society to anyone

viii

interested in knowing more, genealogical information has generally been removed and some biographies honed and slightly rearranged to highlight the pioneer story. The words have not been changed.

## ABOUT THE COLLECTION

The Pioneer Daughters collection owes its existence to Marie Drew, Chair of the Pioneer Daughters Department of the General Federation of Women's Clubs of South Dakota, who dedicated her life to the project, and to the work of the South Dakota General Federation of Women's Clubs (GFWC), who gathered these stories from every state in the union and around the world, over a 40 year period, under Mrs. Drew's guidance.

"History involves more than books, newspapers, speeches, statistics, diaries, and letters," Marie Drew believed. She wanted to document a different kind of history than the one typically taught in schools. "It has to do with people and what they did, what they thought and how they felt, their joys, their sorrows, and their emotions," she said. Most especially, this intuitive Social Historian wanted to save the stories of women. "We should preserve the histories of those women who came into the state and working shoulder to shoulder with their men carved a wonderful state out of the wide sweeping prairies of Dakota," she felt.

That story was sadly lacking, as the state historian, Will G. Robinson, confessed: "We have a shelf full of ponderous tomes, thirty-two inches in length with over [10,000] biographies of male South Dakotans" but "when it comes to the women who worked along side of the men and frequently made it possible for them to accomplish things which gave them a place in our history, little recognition has been given."

These biographies of South Dakota pioneer women have never been published. Although an edited segment was printed by the State Historical Society in 1966 (Volume XXXIII of *South Dakota Department of History Report and Historical Collections*), the focus was on genealogical information and most of the lively stories were left out, as the Editor acknowledged.

Just what is a pioneer? Given the period of white settlement of South Dakota that extended over sixty years, Mrs. Drew defined a Pioneer Woman as "any woman who was in the territory at the time or before the year 1889, when the State was admitted to the Union. That definition applies to all the East River and the Black Hills counties. In the West River counties, a pioneer woman is any woman who went to that part of the state and lived there when it was opened for settlement." Hence, the collection traces a panorama of pioneering unique to this state that began with horse-and-wagon travel into the Yankton area in the 1860's and 1870's. During the next decade "immigrant cars" brought homesteaders by train to the rich wheat lands east of the river. Finally, "Model T" automobiles carried the possessions of ranchers to the west river country after the turn of the century.

As we celebrate the inclusion in our historical picture of these previously excluded white women, welcoming them and recognizing how much more accurate the story of our past now is with their presence, we become clearer on who else is missing.

These are the *Daughters* of Dakota, the ones who came after. In the Pioneer Daughters collection, and in this volume, there is only a sprinkling of the stories of the *Mothers* of Dakota: the original, the Native American women. We have always had the stories of the Sons of the Prairie, now we have the Daughters, but we will never truly know our history, we who took root in South Dakota, until we know the complete stories of the Mothers and Fathers of Dakota.

Each of the stories in this volume that speaks of friendship or fear or benevolence or sharing with Indians raises the question, how did the Indians experience the same situation? How would a Lakota father, part of a people who never struck their children, respond to a white teacher who "punished" his daughter? What would members of a nation for whom hospitality meant walking right in and making yourselves at home think about members of a nation who had windows that were to be used only for looking out, and doors that were to be knocked on and not entered? To a culture that defined politeness by willingness to take all the food offered to you, practicing "it is more blessed to give than to receive," what confusion was raised by people who preached it, yet expected you to take only one piece of the bread offered to you, and not the whole loaf?

Daughters of Dakota points up the absolute need for the true and accurate story of the Mothers, told in their own words.

## THANKS TO

Bonnie Gardner, whose career with the State Historical Society went full-circle with Pioneer Daughters. She came to work in 1966 to help Will Robinson get the Pioneer Daughters collection ready for publication, and retired on the day this book went to press. She knew the significance of the collection, and carefully organized and tended it for over thirty years as it grew. She also helped enormously in the creation of the book.

Barbara Wilkens, who was President of the General Federation of Women's Clubs of South Dakota when I first approached the organization about publishing a book, has been present and supportive in each moment and aspect as the project has grown. Lila Sloat and the current GFWC President, Doris Roden, have been generous with advice and support along the way. My admiration for this organization's long history of civic betterment, of which the Pioneer Daughters project was just one part, has blossomed in the course of my work with them.

Lo Ross, the Research Associate for both the book and Curriculum Unit projects, brought the voices of these pioneer women to life during a long Pierre winter of careful reading of their words, discovering the categories of the experiences they described, and suggesting possible stories.

The friendly and helpful staff at the South Dakota Historical Society, with fresh donuts and hot tea and a willingness to drop everything and help out, made the research a joy.

I'm grateful for the encouragement, support and assistance of many people on this project, including: Jim Larson, Executive Director of the South Dakota Centennial Commission; Alice Kundert, one of the finest historians in the state; Clara Gustafson, Historian of the GFWC; Linda

Sommer, State Archivist; Margo Neuhauser, former Director, S.D. Equal Educational Opportunities Office; Judy Richards, Equity Supervisor, S.D. Office of Adult, Vocational and Technical Education; and Char Madsen, Black Hills Special Services Cooperative.

And finally, thanks to the women who told their stories.

# INTRODUCTION

"Homesteads for Women" headlined an article by Kate Carnes in a popular 1890 journal. Women "may acquire, by a few years of intelligent industry and patient frugality, independence, if not wealth," the author promised.

This was no news to South Dakota women, who held more than one-third of the land in Dakota Territory on the eve of statehood in the late 1880's. Single women and widows who were heads of families flocked to the area, looking for a way to support themselves, build a nest egg, and sometimes find adventure. Carnes suggested to women settlers that they claim homesteads on adjoining land, then build a house on the dividing line between the tracts, a practice which Dakota wives and husbands practiced as well.

Dakota—heralded as "the home of the free and the land of the boomer"—attracted an estimated 200,000 settlers in the years 1880-1883 alone. "In 1883 the cry of Free Land was heard ringing around the world and they decided that they, too, with their family should take advantage of this offer of land to be had just for making some improvements and living on it," explained one Pioneer Daughter. "Where four years ago, the coyote's shrill howl was the refrain of the wilderness, today stand towns of three thousand inhabitants," exulted the developers.

The black, sandy loam with water-retaining clay subsoil brought forth 20 bushels of wheat to the acre. The 50 bushels of corn yield promised that cattle and hogs would flourish on the prairies where bleaching bones of millions of buffalo afforded additional proof to the settlers of the land's friendliness to livestock.

"The climate is dry, clear, and invigorating," with "less sickness in portion to population, than any other State or Territory of the Union," promised the boomers, and many a pioneer came West for their health.

Government land, 160 acres of it, was available to men and women citizens under the Homestead law of 1862 for less than $10 in filing fees if they would live on and farm the land for five years.

Veterans of the Civil War were entitled to use all three rights under the Homestead Law in filing on Government land: a homestead right, a preemption right and a tree claim right. Their time served in the Union army was deducted from the five years needed to prove up on a homestead. Settlers with money could prove-up anytime after six months residence under the Pre-emption law by paying $1.25 an acre for land forty miles from the railroad, or $2.50 an acre for land within that distance.

A tree claim required that the settler plant trees and keep them cultivated and in good growing condition for eight years. If at the end of that time, they could show 6,750 healthy trees, the land was theirs upon paying $4.00 in land office fees. John Pickler, the first Congressman-at-large elected after statehood, got the law amended to accept intent after the first drought destroyed the young saplings. The secret to land acquisition was to start with a pre-emption claim before the railroad came, so you could pay the lower fee. Six months later, you could file your homestead claim, which took longer to prove-up, and finally your tree claim. In less than ten years, you'd have 480 acres of land, and hopefully the railroad would be built near your homestead by then, increasing the land value.

Those who feared that government land would run out had nothing to worry about, for speculators early had their eyes on the Great Sioux Reservation west of the river, which they had every intention of speedily opening to development, regardless of existing treaties with the Indians. In the Black Hills, the government had already more than proven its willingness to violate treaties over lands that speculators wanted. While it was a time of losing land and a way of life for the native people, it was a time of massive expansion for the non-Indian settlers.

Women came to Dakota Territory with their husbands, parents, friends, children and by themselves. These land-holding women carried the confidence that comes with financial independence, combined with a strong interest in the formative conditions of their territory (and later, state), such as the location of school houses and county seats, which affected women's interest as land holders to the same extent as the men. "There are peculiar reasons why our women should have their rights," John Pickler argued when he introduced a woman suffrage bill into the territorial legislature in 1885, "as they own fully one-fourth of the land and are veritable heroines."

The best of the pioneering experiences for women clearly was the one based on their choice to come West. Settlement patterns often involved groups of families and friends uprooting in one location and moving together to a location in Dakota. Town women unpacked their china and immediately began having teas, picking up their social life without losing a stitch. As one Pioneer Daughter put it,

*"Life for a woman in a county seat town, population one thousand, was lived in a leisurely, well regulated manner. There were literary societies, church affairs, lodges and other groups for the betterment of the citizen; and there was always the close companionship of the family."*

At the other end of the spectrum was the wife who experienced being taken from her women-folks and friends and brought to an isolated soddie in a God-forsaken treeless country where extremes in temperature matched natural disasters and loneliness for creating misery and despair. Madness was a not uncommon reaction of these women.

But these are the extremes of experience; certainly there were women who felt both the self-determination and the loneliness of pioneering. Pioneer Daughter stories summarize that complexity:

*"Mrs. Shaykett's life on the river ranch to which her husband took her was that of practically all pioneer women. Much work with many inconveniences. But no complaints were heard. Difficulties were made light of, obstacles laughed away. Dry seasons and short crops sometimes made the jam on the bread very thin, and thread-bare clothing had to be mended until it was often patch upon patch. But these things meant little to those sturdy pioneers who calmly went on their way doing their homely daily duties with no moanings over the hardships of the present and ever supreme hope for the future."*

and

*"Had these optimistic and industrious settlers started with stock raising rather than with plowing up the native*

*soil, the story might have been a happier one. Drought, insects, hail storms, hot winds, and the ever-present prairie fire menace preyed upon and destroyed crops and saplings year after year. The blizzard of 1888 took its toll of lives of both people and stock, while the prairie fire of 1889 left many of our neighbors sitting on bare, burnt-over ground — their homes, their possessions, and their pasture destroyed!!"*

Not surprisingly, many settlers left. Perhaps surprisingly, many homesteaded several times within the state, each time further West as new Indian land was taken.

Why did they come? The Pioneer Daughters collection contains some answers:

*"As we see it now, all had one thing in common. They were either getting away from something or trying to get something. Many were seeking escape from poverty, monotony, or the law. Others left their families and homes to follow a dream the hung like a bright star just out of their reach in the purpling skies of the great mid-west."*

*"Some persons pioneered because they were failures in their home communities, others turned west when the spirit of adventure burned in hearts, souls and minds of a young man and woman. For this two it was the latter — they were fired with enthusiasm to conquer the new frontier."*

Railroads sent agents to Europe with glowing reports of the land and promising free one-way tickets to the Territory. Once the settlers arrived, they found that they had only one way to get their produce to the market — by these same railroads. With no competition or government control, the railroads charged all the traffic would allow — and then some. Republican Congressman John Pickler believed, "It is not fair that the president of a railroad company receive $25,000 to $50,000 per year and then have the companies bleed the producing classes with exorbitant freight rates to pay them."

Banks, who had invested twenty-five million dollars in these western states, charged the farmers up to 20% interest to borrow money to buy the seed and machinery necessary to farm. Many settlers came with little more than the clothes on their back, and were at the mercy of the moneylenders. Pickler objected, "Homesteaders contracted debts for seed grain, tools and teams. Because they bought on credit, they paid unconscionable prices."

Certainly, the railroads, banks and land speculators stood ready to reap great profits off the pioneers, which explains the massive advertising campaign that lured the unwary pioneers to a promised land of milk and honey which didn't always materialize. When the banks and the railroads didn't break a farmer, weather and natural disasters might.

Still, these women were not victims. Subjected, many of them, to conditions beyond endurance, somehow they endured. And left a legacy. As their children later recorded in the Pioneer Daughters collection:

*"More than forty years have passed since my mother went on to that better world and as I think of the comfortable life which is so largely the rule now, I hope Heaven makes up to those pioneer women for the hardships of their lives on the bleak prairies of early days. The monotony of the prairies, the constant struggle against the elements for a livelihood, the paucity of social and intellectual contacts to women gently reared, the fear of fire, blizzard and drought; the white-covered wagons, containing dear neighbors who had given up the struggle there and were trekking on to new endeavors elsewhere—all this was the lot of our pioneer mothers.*

*But, on the other hand, sleigh rides and skating in winter, languorous Indian summer days, gorgeous sunrises and sunsets, the first bluebell in spring and the song of the meadow-lark over the prairie—these were compensations."*

and

*"What constitutes a pioneer woman? The fact that she came to Dakota in pre-statehood days? That she endured the hardships of a virtually new country, where there were terrific blizzards, and equally terrifically hot suns blasting down on the prairies? That there was danger from Indian uprisings? That life was constantly a struggle, and children were born with only a midwife in attendance?*

*No. It seems to me that the chief attribute of a pioneer woman is the fact that she has been able to make of the primitive and hard existence of her early days, a life of beauty and serenity, a life of service to her family and her friends, and a love of all things good and true and beautiful."*

xvii

# Eva L. Ash
## Lawrence County
## 1876

Eva L. Ash (Mrs. Henry), and two children went to the Black Hills with the first train of covered wagons to cross the Indian reservation after the Custer massacre, [battle] which occurred in June, 1876. They came by train from Wisconsin to Yankton, Dakota Territory, and waited at Yankton until a party was formed to start to the Black Hills. They went up the Missouri River from Yankton on the steamer "Yellowstone," leaving Yankton July 29, 1876, and arriving at Fort Pierre the next morning.

While in Yankton Mrs. Ash and children stopped at the old Ash Hotel, whose proprietor was also a Henry Ash, but no relation. Mrs. Ash's husband had also stopped at the same hotel earlier, while on his way to the Black Hills.

They left Yankton about ten in the morning but after a few hours were turned back by a message that there were army supplies that must go forward at once. So the boat was returned to Yankton, and as soon as the freight was loaded they again began the trip. Later the same day the boat ran aground on one of the many sand bars in the Missouri river, and was there until the next morning, when it was freed.

Arriving at Fort Pierre they found over one hundred wagons and several hundred men waiting to start to the Hills. This was the first train of covered wagons to make the trip across the Indian reservation after the Custer massacre, as the government had issued orders that no train of less than one hundred wagons could leave for the Hills at that time, because of Indian trouble.

The men spent the rest of the day moving the freight from the steamer to the ox-drawn, covered wagons, and in preparing the wagons for the families going to the Hills.

When they stopped for the night the wagons carrying the families were the first to stop, the tents were pitched and the train went into camp in a circle around them. The wagons formed a circle with the wagon tongues on the inside and so close together that it would have been almost impossible to pass between them. The horses and other animals were inside the enclosure, and men were stationed to watch for Indians from sundown till sunrise. As soon as supper was over the fires were extinguished so as not to be seen by Indians.

"Calamity Jane," Indian scout and pioneer character, traveled with the same outfit but not with the families; she traveled with the freighters and lived among the men as one of them and it is said that they did not know that she was a woman, but thought her a young lad.

Mrs. Ash said the first few hours of the trip were very pleasant, and the novelty of riding in a covered wagon was enjoyed by the children and many of the older ones also. But before long they ran into a strip where there had been heavy rains, and where some of the party had their first experience with gumbo. Here, indeed, did the work begin. The wagons would go as far as possible, because of gumbo collecting on the wagon wheels — then they would stop, the men get out and shovel gumbo, and the train would move again as far as possible, when the operation would have to be repeated. This continued until late in the afternoon, when they covered the strip where the rains had been heavy.

Henry Ash had gone earlier, in May, 1876, and was waiting for his family at Crook City, twelve miles from Deadwood, where he operated a grocery store (one of the first in the Black Hills) in a large log cabin, selling "sowbelly," sorghum, navy beans, sugar, coffee, strychnine (to kill wolves), quicksilver, etc. He did a thriving business. He remained in Crook until his death in June, 1882.

Mrs. Ash arrived at Crook City August 19, 1876. Soon after the family arrived a bakery was added to the grocery business. She baked on an average, a sack of flour each day, and kneaded the dough in a deep trough against one end of the kitchen wall. She used two large ovens, one built out of doors, of rock, about six feet long and four wide, and rounded over the top like an old fashioned cellar. Another oven was built later of brick across one end of the kitchen. Fires were built inside these ovens by placing huge logs in them, and when the logs had burned, the ashes were raked out, and pans and pans of bread put in to bake. Mrs. Ash had so regulated the heat that she could tell almost to a minute how long it would take the bread to bake.

Wearing a calico dress, with high bosom, slender waist, full skirt almost to the floor, covering high top button shoes, which took precious time each morning to button, she was a handsome woman, five feet, five inches tall, daintily rounded, with a wealth of dark brown hair, worn at the nape of her neck, grey eyes, clear, healthy complexion and regular features.

The bakery was a success and Mr. and Mrs. Ash then added a large log cabin hotel. This hotel was a busy place. One of the stage coaches stopped there, carrying numerous passengers, among whom was Mrs. Mary Eddy Baker, the Christian Science leader, who stopped on one or two occasions, while on her way to visit her son, George Glover, at Lead City.

There were many Indian scares in those early days. The Indians often came down to the edge of the settlement and drove away horses and other animals before the men could get their guns. On two occasions women and children were rushed to a central cabin and men armed the rifle pits. A Major Whitehead was in command of a cannon and a large pile of canisters. Everything was done to protect the women and children if the Indians came. The men made ready to meet the Indians if they attacked the settlement. At another time three men were attacked by Indians and one of the men was scalped, another killed.

Most of the meat used at that time was wild game: buffalo, elk, deer, and bear. Food in those days consisted largely of "sowbelly" flapjacks, navy beans, dried apples, coffee, and some canned vegetables and wild game; antelope sold at 15 cents a pound; potatoes, 25 cents; mustard, 1 dollar; soap, 25 cents a cake; baking powder, 50 cents a pound; onions, 15 cents; canned corn, 40 cents; flour sold at from $12 to $50 a 50 lb. sack, and only 10 pounds to a customer much of the time. Five pounds of sugar cost $1.00, Arbuckle coffee from 40 cents to 60 cents. Because of the deep snows it was often six weeks from the time one freight train got through until the next one arrived.

There were no cats in the Hills for several years and a mouse trap cost 50 cents. When a man came later with a load of cats, Mrs. Ash paid $5 for a common alley cat, later buying another.

Mail was carried by horseback and 50 cents was paid for each letter received. One of the mail carriers, Charlie Nolin, traveled with the same ox-drawn covered wagon train that took Mrs. Ash to the Hills, joining it a few miles from Fort Pierre, after trailing them for some time to be sure they were not Indians. He stayed with the party until they reached Rapid City, then a village of twelve log cabins, when he left them to go on alone. The next morning his body was found stretched across the road with three pieces of scalp taken; the mail sacks had been ripped open and the contents scattered to the four winds.

Fireplaces were used almost entirely, but Mrs. Ash had a large, heavy iron range and for cooking she used heavy iron kettles, which were set down upon the hot coals. She used a heavy iron tea kettle, which weighed several pounds, for heating water, and she also had a large reservoir on the back of the range.

One winter, because of a shortage, kerosene was sold at from one dollar to one dollar and fifty cents a gallon. Mrs. Ash often molded and used tallow candles.

She had many things to contend with in getting help at the hotel. There were few women there and they were busy at home. At one time she had a Chinese man to do the laundry, mop floors, and carry water and wood. There was no coal and wood was used entirely. Another time she had colored help; later a Norwegian girl who ran away and married a gambler. Still a little later she employed two strong German girls who could not speak a word of English and Mrs. Ash could not speak German, but by numerous gestures and occasionally calling on Mr. Ash to interpret, she managed to teach them what she wanted them to do, and they became very good assistants. They were good girls; one of them married a prosperous German farmer and her descendants still live in the Hills. The other girl continued to help at the hotel for some time.

The stage coach which stopped at the hotel was often late in getting in, and sometimes Mrs. Ash would have to get supper at ten o'clock at night. Crook City was the last stop before getting to Deadwood, twelve miles distant. One night when the stage stopped as usual, among the passengers was an Indian being taken to Deadwood for trial, one of the first Indians to stand trial for killing a white man. The Indians were so incensed that it was feared that they might follow the stage coach and massacre the passengers if they stopped for supper. The driver stopped long enough to explain the circumstances and hurried on to Deadwood, where the Indian was put in custody of the sheriff.

Mrs. Ash, at one time, had suffered with a severe toothache for several days. There was no dentist in town. On the coach which drove in and stopped, so that the passengers could get dinner, was a medical doctor. Mr. Ash asked the M.D. to pull the offending tooth for his wife. The doctor had nothing with him to deaden the pain, but nevertheless, Mrs. Ash sat down on an ordinary straight back chair, and the doctor extracted thirteen teeth. As soon as the bleeding stopped she went to the kitchen and helped serve the meal.

One night some time after her husband's death Mrs. Ash heard loud voices and shooting. Looking out of her upstairs window she saw in the bright moon light, a man hanging from a limb of a tree on the hillside, and heard and saw his body riddled by bullets. She soon realized that this was another "necktie party."

The victim had robbed and beaten an old man and left him for dead, but other men passing heard his cries and helped the old man to town; a vigilance committee was formed, and found the young man in a gambling house with money on him, put a rope around his neck, and led him to the nearest tree.

For many nights Mrs. Ash could not close her eyes without again seeing the gruesome sight. This was one of the numerous incidents which occurred during the life of the early day pioneer.

In the early days many families came to the Hills with just enough money to reach their destination. Mr. Ash was always glad to "carry" an account for a man, at the grocery store, until he could plant and grow a crop, when he was expected to pay for the accommodation as soon as possible.

The miners paid their way as fast as they could dig the
gold from the ground, but the farmers had to wait until
nature did her share, before they could pay. Mr. Ash was
lenient, and seldom took a mortgage or any form of protection, as it was not necessary in most cases, as a man
soon found that if he did not pay his debts, he did not
eat long after.

After her husband's death Mrs. Ash sold the grocery
store, and tried to collect the accounts. There was an abundant potato crop that year, and during the fall she asked
one big German farmer to pay his account, $500. She told
him if he did not have the money to pay he could bring
her potatoes to apply on the account, and also other
vegetables, which she could use in the hotel. His reply was
that, "He would pay no damned woman." "If Henry was alive
he would pay him, but he would not pay a woman."

It was said that this man was in the habit of beating
his wife at times. One night men dressed in white sheets
gathered at his home and called him out. They told him
they had come to hang him for beating his wife, and that
women were treated with respect in this country. He was
so frightened that he got down on his knees and begged
for his life. This was done only to frighten him, and to teach
him a lesson.

In those far away days Mrs. Ash had young strength
in her arms and back and pride and ambition in her heart.
She was years younger than her husband and was left a
widow at twenty-eight, with three children, one a baby boy
eleven days old, at the time of her husband's death.

Mrs. Ash lived in Crook and the Hills for many years.
She remained a widow fifty-one years.

# Aase Aslakson
## Kingsbury County
## 1879

*[Aase was 87 years of age and living in Waubay, South Dakota when she told this story of her life. It was translated from Scandinavian February 12, 1950.]*

I was born in Norway on May 16, 1863. My parents were very poor, so, at the age of eight, I left home to make my own way in the world. I had to herd cattle and sheep and had very little schooling. I learned to write by drawing letters in the dirt with a long stick, while herding cattle. This was hard for me. I cried every day for the first year, I believe. The people I worked for lived near Telemarken, then I went to Vegossia-Myre where I herded for 3 more years. Things went better as I grew older. The rain often lasted for days and when it came time to go home the ravines were flooded so I waded through and carried the lambs to the shore. The man who did the most for me after I left home was Erick Myre. He was a true Christian and supplied all my school needs, even paper and pencils without my asking. How often I've wept because I didn't thank him the way I should have, but I was young and didn't understand. He was my teacher and I stayed in his home. When I was ill, he would lead me by the hand to the stove, and help do my lessons for me. For this, he has not received any reward. He is home with Jesus now, that I know.

Then came the time when I became a hired girl. This was a very hard place. I was up early in the morning and worked late into the night. It was my job to spin and weave and after dark the wool had to be carded. The coal had to be gathered in the woods. This was hard because we had to be up at night and watch the coal as it went through the burning process. For three hours every nite I carried water, then someone would come and take my place. I was so tired I slept with my clothes on even though they were covered with ice. While doing this work, I contracted asthma which bothers me to this day. I stayed there for two years and in April of the second year my ticket came from America. My brother, Peter, and my sister, Bertha, went with me. It was a long, rough trip across the Atlantic.

After reaching America I went to Volga, South Dakota where some of my folks lived. This was in 1879. I was not well, and there was always the heavy burden in my heart. I was lonesome for Norway! I left my relatives that first summer and again was herding cattle. As far as I could see, there was nothing but some sod houses and prairie. This was so different from my homeland. It was terrible. I was such a stranger and I did not understand the language. When I went to bed at night, I wept until I fell asleep. I worked in Brookings at the Morehouse hotel until Christmas, then went to my brother's place where I was married Feb. 14, 1882. We lived at Brookings for fifteen years and six of my children were born there. We moved to a farm south of Waubay in Day County. Just previous to this, our house in Brookings burned. Fire started in the kitchen, where we burned flax-straw. My mother threw all her clothes out of the upstairs window, then she jumped from the same window.

In 1900 we again lost our house by fire. My mother was home alone and when we got there, I ran into the house and stumbled over her unconscious body and succeeded in dragging her out of the building. We took her to our nearest neighbor, Bill Hayden, where she stayed for a week. We used egg whites night and day but she recovered without a Doctor. We stayed at Uncle Olson's place for six weeks, then we got a one room house built.

We lived nine miles south of Waubay for many years. At this farm home I weathered many a storm and faced many disappointments but it seems to have been the best part of my life, because the children were home. When the last one left, it seemed dark but "He does all things well." All lives must be filled with blessings and disappointments. I thank God for everything.

Finally sold the farm and bought a home in Waubay where I take comfort. I am now 87, my journey soon ended.

Early in the summer of '46 I fell and broke my hip. I was taken to the Webster hospital, with my leg in a cast, suspended from the ceiling, for seven weeks. I was supposed to stay in that position for 8 weeks but at the end of seven weeks I could stand it no longer, so I took a small pocket-knife from my purse and cut the string. Down my leg came with a thud. I rolled out of bed and tried to walk but, of course, I fell. Doctors and nurses came running from every direction and, for once, I got a lot of attention. I am happy to say that my hip and leg are all well again and I can walk some without my cane.

# Hettie Elsie Ferguson Bable
## Beadle County
## 1886

**Written by Mrs. Bable in 1949**

*[Born February 9, 1866, in Blackberry, Kane County, Illinois, her parents moved to Polk County, Iowa when Hettie was two years old. A middle child in a family of twelve, she followed two of her older sisters to Dakota Territory, marrying her sister Sarah's brother-in-law after meeting him on a trip to the Territory in 1886. Hettie's oldest sister Nettie lived in Hyde County.]*

In November of 1887 my husband and I drove overland from Hitchcock to sister Nettie's home north of Highmore, a distance of eighty miles, for a week's visit. After our return we received a letter from my mother sternly admonishing us for making such a trip at that time of the year. Nothing happened to mar the pleasure of the trip but on the day after our arrival at home a storm hit us.

January 12th is more than a date to all who were living in Dakota Territory in 1888. We were well housed and comfortable but the great blizzard that swept over the state caused no little concern for me. I knew that sister Nettie was awaiting a visit from Mr. Stork, by the way his fifth trip to her home, and the knowledge of his visit and away out on the prairie, miles from neighbors and no doctor closer than Highmore, a blizzard raging and the thermometer dropping, didn't do anything to one's peace of mind. A baby daughter was born on January 21st.

That year passed with nothing exceptional happening but for a few of the less hardy homesteaders packing up and going back home.

Spring came early in 1889. Most of the field work was completed and I had my house-cleaning done and the heating stove taken out by April 1, so that on the morning of April 3 when a strong wind blowing out of the northwest brought a disagreeable chilliness, the only heat I had was from the gasoline stove oven. To conserve fuel I baked cookies, pies, bread and rolls. The wind made me uneasy and there was a tense feeling in the atmosphere, as though something were about to happen. The air began to fill with smoke, apparently from numerous small local prairie fires or burning straw stacks.

Late in the afternoon of the same day my husband and I called on a neighbor and when we returned home at about seven o'clock, we found a telegram from sister Nettie's father-in-law, stating that a prairie fire the day before had destroyed all of their buildings and livestock, and Frank, the oldest son, had died from burns and sister Nettie was not expected to live.

Train service was not too good and not knowing just what transportation facilities would be available at Highmore, we decided to again make the long trip by team and buggy.

The horses had been in the field all day and had to have rest before starting on the eighty-mile trek across the uncharted prairie. At two o'clock in the morning of April 4 we began the journey. At about two o'clock in the afternoon we reached the scene of the fire. Charred ruins of what had been home, dead cattle and hogs, was all that was left.

When we saw that everything was destroyed we headed for Highmore, twenty miles away. The horses were near exhaustion but we urged them on and reached town late in the afternoon. There we met my brother-in-law and the friends and neighbors returning from the cemetery where they had just buried my sister and her son. Nettie had passed away before the telegram had reached me.

Tom Tibbs, my brother-in-law, was badly burned and suffering from shock. His wife and son dead, everything he possessed in worldly goods gone, and four little motherless children, one a baby girl fourteen months old, to care for.

Mr. Babel stayed in Highmore until the following Tuesday when, in company with the eldest child, a girl of six, he returned to Hitchcock with the horses and buggy. My father had arrived from Iowa and we took the two youngest children home with us. When my father returned to Iowa the youngest boy went with him and remained there until he was ten years old. I kept the others: Mazie, six years old; Elza, four; and Dolly, a little over one year old; until January 1890, when Mazie went to the home of my sister and the boy returned to live with his father. I kept the baby until she was a young lady.

If you were to drive north and a little west of Highmore you could still see the rock foundation that once was the barn that housed the stock that might have been the beginning of a livelihood for a young and ambitious couple, planning for the future of their little family. A grim reminder of a careless action or a deliberate crime.

# Pearl Badger
## Native American
### 1871

Mrs. Badger, a full-blood [Dakota] Indian woman, was born in a tepee in the fall of 1871. Neither her father nor mother spoke any language other than Dakota.

In her early teens, she was selected as one of a group of outstanding Indian youths and was taken to Carlyle Indian School at Carlyle, Pennsylvania. After completing her education there, she returned to Fort Thompson where she married Henry Badger. He is remembered as one of the superb horsemen of the Crow Creek area. She had told friends her husband paid seven ponies, some silver and a piece of land for her. Mrs. Badger was considered an outstanding artisan and dancer.

Dr. Roscoe E. Dean, who was Mrs. Badger's physician during her later years, reported she was a very proud person who would speak in English to only a few of her white friends and as far as he knows, she never accepted any white person as her equal.

In spite of a close working relationship and many visits, Mrs. Badger would only speak in general terms of the difficult years when she was a small girl.

When questioned about something which might reveal secrets connected with Indian raids, Mrs. Badger would inevitably pretend not to understand. An example was one occasion when she was questioned about the Wessington incident. Legend has it that the trapper, Wessington, was burned at the stake in the Wessington Hills by Indians. There is no question that she knew something of the incident, but with a flicker of a smile, she pretended not to understand the question. She would answer in the Dakota language when an attempt was made to visit with her for several days following this.

13

Mrs. Badger was one of the older Indians who prefer to be known as members of the Yankton tribe and the Dakota Nation. She was insulted when she was referred to as a Sioux which loosely translated means "cut-head."

## "Early Experiences on a South Dakota Farm"
## Margaret Heil Becker
## Dewey County
## 1917

In 1917 I moved to South Dakota from North Dakota with my parents, the Jacob Heils. My Grandmother had passed away and as my Mother was an only child, she felt she had to come out and help Grandpa. At the time I was twelve years old, never having lived on a farm, much less way out on the prairie. Times were hard. My Dad was a grain elevator manager in North Dakota and farming came hard for him.

I can remember the first summer we were on the farm we had a real good crop. Wheat was cut with a binder at that time. I was sent out alone to shock grain on a forty-acre field. You can imagine how fast the binder got away from me. I'd set up a shock, sit down and cry, and go again. I remember an old Indian man named Charlie Face came by and pitched in and could he shock grain! At that time my folks didn't know Indian people very well and they said he had to come in to eat. After he'd eaten his fill, he went home and again I was left alone. The next day both Mom and Dad came out and the grain was soon shocked.

But about our trip out here. My mother and six of us children came before Dad. My older sister stayed with Dad. When we got to Eagle Butte, we had to stay in the only hotel. My mother was afraid of bedbugs so we slept in our clothes. The next day Mr. Naeve took us in his Model T twelve miles to the farm. About half-way, a creek had to be crossed. We all had to get out while he drove across and then we waded across and went on.

The first year when they had the Indian Fair, the Indians would come past our place, a caravan maybe two miles long: wagons, horses and what have you. We kids didn't get to go to town to the fair as it was too far.

One thing I remember is taking grain in a three-top wagon box with four horses to town to sell the grain and bring back winter supplies. I had to drive one wagon when I was about fourteen years old and at the time we had a high hill that we called High Elk Hill, and believe me, coming down that hill was no fun with a load, but somehow I got down without mishap but with lots of praying.

# Susan Bordeaux Bettelyoun
## Tripp County
## 1857

by Susan Bordeaux Bettelyoun
as told to Carol Case Goddard
Republished in the *Tripp County Journal* March 7, 1940

I, Susan Bordeaux Bettelyoun, was born March 15, 1857, the sixth of eleven children born to James Bordeaux and his wife Huntkalutawin, a full-blooded Brule Indian woman. We children all received a fair education, far above the average for children in those early days.

In 1891 I married Issac P. Bettelyoun, a scout and interpreter for the government. He was later in the battle [massacre] of Wounded Knee and died in 1934 at the soldier's home in Hot Springs.

My father was a very proud man and yet a most modest one. He never wanted to give his frontier life and experiences to any publishers or writers while he was living. No one has ever published this experience he had with "Pete" on Bear Butte, nor is it generally known. My father was a wonderful man and devoted to my mother and to us children. He was respected and well thought of by both whites and Indians. Father died in 1878 and is buried at Rosebud Spotted Tail Agency. My mother died six years later, at the age of 63 years, and is buried beside him.

I will be 83 years old the 15th of March. The rest of my days I want to spend in writing my experiences, early day history of the Sioux Indians fighting the government for their country, and of the many Indian battles with the soldiers which I saw with my own eyes.

I first saw Bear Butte in 1910. I had wanted to see it as I had often heard my father tell about it. My husband, Isaac Bettelyoun, and I were on White Rocks in Deadwood and I said, "What butte is that?"

"Why, that is Bear Butte," my husband replied. I suddenly started to cry and he thought I was ill. It came to me so overwhelmingly all that my poor father had endured and gone through, and he so young, that I cried for him.

## A STORY OF BEAR BUTTE

Paul and Felix Bordeaux came to the United States from France in the early 19th century, about 1814. The Bordeaux family belonged to the aristocrats and had owned land where the city of Bordeau now stands. Paul was my grandfather and Felix was his brother. The brothers landed in New Orleans, later going to St. Louis, and Felix continued on up the Mississippi to its source. My grandfather returned to France and brought back his French wife, Margaret Louise. They settled in St. Louis, in that part of Louisiana territory which became, in 1821, the state of Missouri.

My father, James Bordeaux, was born in St. Louis in 1818, the eldest son of Paul and Margaret Louise Bordeaux. My father was very ambitious and started out for himself when only a boy. John Jacob Astor had opened a western branch office of the American Fur Company at St. Louis in 1819 and although father was but fifteen years old, he got a position with them at one of their western posts.

Father left St. Louis in 1833, "the years when the stars fell," headed for the American Fur Company post (later called Ft. Union) at the mouth of the Yellowstone River where it empties into the Missouri River. According to the Indian winter count and the Indian hieroglyphic calendar and record, it rained stars that year. His work at the post consisted mainly of stretching beaver pelts on large rings to dry. The pelts were bought by weight and because the white trappers often rubbed the moist green pelts with white sand to make them heavy, the company purchased their supply chiefly from the Indians.

### To South Dakota

In 1836, my father left the post, still in the employ of the American Fur Company, accompanied by "Pete," his pardner (also in their employ) and started toward what is now

Fort Laramie, but then known only as the American Fur
Company stockade. They carried a small bundle of letters,
the United States mail, destined for the stockade. Probably
that was the earliest mail carried across what is now the
state of South Dakota.

Father and "Pete" had to go afoot because they were
afraid of the Indians. Father never mentioned "Pete's" last
name as I recall. We knew him just as "Pete." They traveled
at night and hid in the woods during the day time. They
carried very little equipment, only a small pack containing
food, a blanket and extra pair of shoes and some moccasins,
a muzzleloader and a big pistol for each—and the packet
of mail.

When they got to Bear Butte, which in those days was
thickly timbered and inhabited by numerous black bears,
a tribe of Ree Indians set upon them. It was early morning.
Father said that the Rees trailed them like hounds, following
them up the steep mountain sides until finally it became
so rocky and steep the Rees had great difficulty pursuing
them. "Pete" paused, reloaded his gun, and fired at them.
The Rees turned and fled in terror, but not before "Pete"
had been shot with an arrow in the back, close to the spine.

My father and "Pete" kept on climbing until they reached
the top of the mountain where there was a cold spring. Father
had seen the Indians make their poisoned arrows on other
occasions and knew at once that it was a poisoned arrow
that had struck his pardner, for his body began to swell
up and he was in terrible agony. All day father kept putting
cold water on "Pete's" wound and feverish body, the skin
continued to puff up all over, and they both knew he was
going to die. "Pete" lived until sundown and suffered horribly.

### Prepare for Death

Before "Pete" died, he wrote a letter to the American
Fur Company telling them to give his wages to my father,
that he had been shot by the Rees and was going to die
with a poisoned arrow. When "Pete" lay dying there on top
of Bear Butte he also told my father to: "Take my shoes
and moccasins, because I am afraid you will get lost or
something will happen to you and you will need them." Before
he died, he also made my father promise to put his body

in a cave along the ledge near the top of the mountain and
to cover his body with big slabs of stone so no animals
could come and get him. He also requested that father take
the poisoned arrow and put it in his hand so that when
his own father came to claim his body, as was the custom
for the parents of wealthy Frenchmen slain in the West,
he would know what had killed his son. Father did as "Pete"
had asked him, concealing the body in the cave which was
near the springs on top of the mountain. While on Bear
Butte with "Pete" that day father said a storm passed under
them and they could see the lightening, but could not hear
the thunder.

Father went on alone after his pardner was killed and
finally reached the American Fur Company's stockade, at
what is now known as Fort Laramie, with the packet of letters.

"Pete's" father couldn't come to get his son's body until
two years afterwards, in 1838. In spite of being seen by
the Indians and attacked, they rode horseback this time.
They left the horses at the base of the mountain and both
climbed afoot. Father guided "Pete's" father to the cave where
his son's body was hidden. They had no trouble finding the
place. Everything was just as father had left it and "Pete's"
father was overjoyed to find nothing had been disturbed,
though, of course, the clothes and flesh had fallen away from
the bones. Still clutched in "Pete's" hand was the poisoned
arrow. They put "Pete's" bones in a sack and carried them
horseback to the American Fur company stockade.

It is possible that "Pete" was buried in the old Jesuit
Catholic cemetery in St. Louis, because they used to take
the bodies of slain Frenchman back there and it was the
earliest cemetery in St. Louis.

## Bear Butte

My father told me that in the early days when he first
saw Bear Butte it was heavily timbered. It seemed almost
unbelievable to me that the mountain could be the same
mountain father had told me about for it looked so barren,
but I am very sure it was, for father, in telling of his experience with "Pete" and the Rees, always called it Bear Butte,
or the Indian name for it, Mato Paha, which he said had
been given to it by the Sioux. Also he recalled seeing a

quartz lode there with a gold vein clearly visible to the naked eye. I suppose now it has all eroded away. I recall distinctly that father told me it was a mountain by itself, way off from the rest of the Black Hills.

Some people have the mistaken idea that the mountain was called Bear Butte because it was so barren, even though the spelling is "bear" not "bare." Father said it got its name from the prevalence of black bears which lived there, and which were quite common throughout the Black Hills during the greater part of 1800's.

I talked with three Oglala Indians while in Deadwood in 1910 about Bear Butte. I told them that my father had said that it was heavily wooded when he visited it in 1838 and 1840. They said that lightning had struck the butte three times and burned off all the timber and after the third burning it never grew again.

Crazy Hawk, one of the Rosebud Indians, told me that in 1873 he started from the Spotted Tail agency, below Chadron, Nebraska. He left at the time that chokecherries were ripe, going north, so it must have been about the first part of the middle of August. Evidently he must have become sun struck, for he didn't know anything until he found himself on top of Bear Butte. His pony was almost dead with fatigue. He had used a buffalo hide for a saddle blanket and when he took it off the hair on the pony's back fell away. That showed he must have traveled a very long time and been in terrific heat. I talked to him personally in 1906 when I was field matron on the Rosebud reservation and visited his house. He told me that the cold spring was still on top of the butte at that time, but the heavy timber had disappeared.

# Christine Kunz Boehler
## Campbell County
### 1883

by her Granddaughter, Nettie Kunz Hauck

The rugged 21-day covered wagon trip from Yankton to the farm eight miles north of Java, on which Christine had originally filed a claim, was one never to be forgotten.

To make the journey to Campbell County to start life anew on virgin soil, in then unsettled country, Christine had to sell her small home in Yankton. Her husband had died in Yankton and to make a living for herself and her two young children meant much hard labor and so the idea of starting life anew elsewhere appealed to her. The small home brought only $100. The sale price was not sufficient to buy a team of oxen, as she had planned, so she used part of the money to purchase a heifer, which would provide milk for her children and made arrangements to make the long journey north with five other families who had made plans to settle in the new territory. A bad snow storm stopped the caravan for two days at Parkston, where the families were hard put to keep warm, due to a short ration of fuel.

They were able to follow wagon trails most of the way from Yankton to Aberdeen, then a village made up of two stores and a depot, but from the Hub City west they broke their own trail. There wasn't even a cowpath.

Immediately upon arrival at their destination, May 29, 1883, rain began to fall and for two solid weeks it poured and drizzled, and drizzled and poured. The families had only their covered wagons for shelter and their only source of fuel for cooking and heat was grass, which they twisted, and dried in the oven of an old cook range which they had brought with them from Yankton.

On the first day after their arrival in Campbell County, Christine and her sister took up the chore of digging a well, since there was no other source of water near. Men in the ❧

party of five families could provide no assistance with this chore, since they had to devote every minute they were not asleep to breaking sod preparatory to planting crops and to get sod with which to build sod houses. Christine and her sister were highly jubilant when on the second day of their digging project they struck water. A few days later the well was complete with rock walls. It still stands today.

As if the task of starting life anew in an unsettled territory wasn't enough of a hardship for a widow and two small children to face in a single year, they were confronted in the fall with a total crop failure. Due to the families' late arrival in the spring, the crops were late and frost got them before they were ready for harvest. The loss included vegetables as well as wheat and corn. Christine and her family went into the winter of 1883 with only 100 pounds of corn meal and 50 pounds of wheat flour, which they purchased in Ipswich, and the milk from their young cow, between them and starvation. Christine fed her children corn mush and milk for dinner and milk and corn mush for supper every day that winter. Cold weather boots for the children's feet were made out of old gunny sacks.

The second winter was a hard one, too. That was the year (1884) of the famous blizzard which many old timers still think was one of the worst this state has ever seen. There was lots of snow, and bitter cold prevailed for weeks at a time. The family had by now, however, added one valuable food to their stock...antelope meat. Antelope were thick in the territory and it was a simple matter to replenish the meat stock during the winter months so long as the dogs found antelope trapped to kill.

More families settled in the vicinity in 1886 and the pioneer atmosphere began to fade. Occasionally a minister would ride out on horseback from Aberdeen and conduct church services, sometimes staying for a week to hold revival meetings.

In 1890, the year Campbell County was organized, Indians had killed the Spenker family near Winona and word had spread that the Indians were on the warpath and were advancing toward the Campbell County settlement. This was about the time Sitting Bull was killed. Communications were a word of mouth proposition in those days and sometimes for lack of authentic information imaginations ran rampant, creating undue alarm and panic for Christine and her two children as well as for the other settlers.

The settlers, 15 families now, gathered in the largest of the sod houses, nailed most of the windows shut and prepared for Indian attacks, with muzzle guns, exhammers and pitchforks as their defense weapons. For three nights they stood guard and on the fourth day a rider came from the West spreading the alarm that the Indians were now on the east side of the river. Wagons were loaded and at 4 p.m. they started to roll at full speed toward Eureka. They found the town crowded with settlers who were there for the same reasons. The railroad had 11 coaches on the track ready to take aboard the women and children in case of emergency.

Many cruel pranksters had their fun during this period of panic and unrest, deliberately spreading false rumors which caused settlers to scurry back and forth between their farm homes and Eureka.

The semiannual treks by ox team to Ipswich were about as lengthy a project in those days as a trip to California would be today. Christine packed a bag of dry bread for her young son before he started on such trips. Nights were spent in sleep under the wagons.

What trying times for poor Christine who often wept bitterly because of loneliness, homesickness and panic, but who never faltered and who never forgot that God was with her. Such faith, such courage, such strength!

# Mable Dora Lee Brownwolf
## Ziebach County
## 1910

*[Born in Missouri in 1905, Mable was five when her father came to South Dakota with several other men, each finding 160 acres of land to claim for homesteading with the assistance of a government surveyor.]*

These same men started from Burlington Junction, Missouri, around the 15th day of April with three wagons of supplies and three or four wagons to haul the people. They left the women and children in Burlington Junction with the promise to see them in Omaha, Nebraska, in a week or less. In five or six days the women loaded the children and what other things such as clothing etc., that they had on the train and headed for Omaha, arriving there that night. They stayed at some hotel the rest of the night.

The following day my mother took my two-year-old brother and myself to noon lunch at the hotel kitchen. I shall never forget that meal if I live to be one hundred years old. My mother told the waiter we wanted fried chicken for our meat. I was to get one wing and one drumstick. The waiter brought our plates, and OH! did the golden brown chicken look good! Being hungry as all children always are, I began on my chicken wing. Breaking the wing apart, I came upon the thing that made this meal unforgettable! The underneath of this wing was covered with feathers, only covered up with browned flour. I was always touchy about my eating so I showed my mother, right then and there. Mother would not let us two eat any more! She called the waiter and asked for her money back, which she got and we ended up eating cold dinner.

Some time that day these women and children joined their husbands with the covered wagons and headed towards South Dakota, going along the east side of the Missouri River up to Wakpala just below Mobridge, South Dakota.

There the seven covered wagon train crossed on a large flat ferry. As near as I can remember, there were two dogs and two cows along with the families. As I recall these four families are all there were in the wagon train.

After crossing the Missouri River, the wagon train headed southwest cross-country, heading for the homesteads which were located seventeen miles southwest of the present town of Dupree. The old Indian trail took these people along the sand hills right south of Eagle Butte. There were no houses or towns below Timber Lake, sixty some miles to the northwest of our trail. On the first day across the unknown plains we encountered many new and interesting things.

One I remember well. The leader of the train put his hand outward in gesture of approaching riders from the southeast. This was on the flat east of present Eagle Butte. These riders were young cowhands of the big Diamond A Cattle Company. They talked English and informed the wagon train occupants no harm was intended, and said for the people to go to the creek for shade and water, but it was too far away. The wagons had one wagon with barrels of water from which they gave the horses a drink every so far. Whenever they came to extra water along the trail they filled the barrels.

Once on the trail again, we soon came in sight of the lonely camper who had been out there with the coyotes and snakes and hawks for about two weeks. Mr. Pidcock had left his oldest son, George, along with a large tent and dog, on the homestead site some weeks before.

It took the wagon train two weeks to travel from Omaha, Nebraska to Wakpala to the camp. We arrived there May 10, 1910, near sundown. It took two days from Wakpala to the camp. After arriving at the camp, the others left this No. 1 camp to go to their own homesteads about a mile in either direction. There they pitched a tent of their own. After two or three days of having no company, a family came over the ridge. It happened to be that day a long sincere friendship began between two different people, so as to speak, myself and the Bridwell girls.

The first real labor my father did on his new home was to dig with a shovel a large nine-feet-deep hole which he called a cave. He traded some of the things he brought from Missouri to Mr. Bridwell and Mr. Owl King and Mr. Ward for poles or logs with which to put a roof over this hole. He put a door one side and steps going to the bottom of the cave. This cave served as our refrigerator and a place to keep our garden stuff for many years to come.

After the horses were rested from the long travel, my dad and the other settlers' menfolks took their teams and wagons up to Timber Lake for fresh supplies. There the men each purchased a sulky plow, a plow drawn by two or four horses and brought it home with them. Then they plowed up the land and cut squares of sod. By placing these sod squares on top of each other they built houses. They put lumber on top for the roof. On top of the boards they put tar paper and put tar over it to keep out the rain. Sometimes they even put a layer of sod on the roof. They even put windows and door frames of lumber purchased from Timber Lake or Isabel. On the inside was blue building paper for covering over the sod, and canvas tents for floor covering. These houses were warm in winter and cool in summer but not very strong, not strong enough to turn a horn of a steer, for example.

There was a large water hole in a slew, about a mile from the house. We had to go down to this water hole to carry water for all our household uses, washing clothes, cooking and so on. On this special day, my mother took my brother and me with her to carry water from the water hole. She had five-gallon pails that she always used to carry water. Mr. Bridwell had warned us all to beware of wild cattle which were numerous around the plains then. He called them Texas longhorns. Well, anyway, we got to the water hole and were just about to reach the top of the hill where our house was. Lo, and behold, Mother heard a bellowing such as those steers made. All at once we saw a lone animal approaching. Mother grabbed my brother and put him a straddle on her side and me on the other side. In each hand she still carried a five-gallon pail of water. She started to run. We have about the distance of a city block to go before we reach the house. We just went around the corner of the house when that steer runs his horn through the corner of the house. The whole corner of our sod house had to be replaced.

There probably is a wandering thought in the mind of
the reader here. To satisfy that — one of the roaming cowboys
just happened through that spot and saw what happened.
He came to the house to see if any one survived. He tried
whipping the steer but finally had to shoot the animal to
get it away.

Next after the house and cave were completed, Dad took
a green willow stick and twitched it in front of him to locate
water. He must have walked the length of seven city blocks
before this stick began to buckle up in his hands. There
with a post hole auger he started to dig a well. He dug
as deep as the auger was long. Then he took a shovel spade
and made a well forty-three feet deep, and six across. He
dug maybe thirty feet and struck a small vein of water coming through a thick layer of blue shale. He took a steel
crowbar and dug thru the shale and there he struck a wonderful big vein of water and it was soft water. He put up a
derrick above the well with a pulley and rope and pail, that
I on top hauled the dirt and slush up and returned the empty pail. Dad stepped in this pail and I hauled him to the
surface. That water kept rising to about 20 or 30 feet. Dad
and I went to another neighbor's place, who had lots of
stony hills around his home. Mr. Birkland was the man's
name. This land is about 10 miles south of Dupree, west
side of the highway and in these hills we dug out blue granite
rock, broke it as we could so Dad could handle it, and hauled
this by horse and wagon to this well. Dad walled this well
from top to bottom with this rock and when finished he
purchased a pump from Isabel and put in this well.

It was in the summer of 1910 that Mr. Frank Barnes
started the town of Dupree. He started in a 12 by 12 tent
with 4 by 8 lumber for the counters. The early settler hauled
Mr. Barnes' supplies by team and wagon from Timber Lake
and Isabel.

In 1912 there was a school house built in a large slew
north of where Ed Ritter placed his homestead home. It
was government land at that time but later became school
land.

About 1915, Dad took another homestead south on Ash
Creek about ten or twelve miles from the first. There were
several homesteads around by then, and another school house

about a mile northwest of home. By this time Dupree had a cafe, hardware, clothing stores, and several other places of business.

There were several invaders into the peaceful life of the early settlers. Mr. Jonas Owl King seemed to be the greatest!! He annoyed the people from Dupree clear to his own brother Albert and residents down along the Rattle Snake Creek.

One time Jonas had every person on each side of the road from Dupree to Rattle Snake Creek just so scared and bewildered beyond words. He, Jonas, had caught a ride into Dupree late one afternoon and decided to go back on foot. He more than likely had come prepared for what he was to undertake. He went to the cafe and gave a hard luck story to the manager. He said that he had a wife and six children at Rattle Snake Creek. His wife was very sick and so were four of his children. He had been unable to work or get anything to eat and they were starving. He asked for food there at the cafe. Well, they gave him bread, meat, potatoes, milk and what not, believing his sad story. He put all of this in a fifty-pound flour sack which he took from under his jacket. He left, then went to the next closest place and he told the same story again. He kept that up for seventeen miles until he came to my father's place.

It was about seven in the evening and my folks were out at the barn doing evening chores. I was alone inside with my brother when a knock was heard. Being just kids, my brother said, "Come in." Jonas was already inside the door and I asked him what he wanted. So he told me a sad story. I told him mother and dad were outside, to wait until they came back. But he said, "No," he was "in a hurry." I told him to sit down. Mother had just roasted a large piece of pork and baked a weeks supply of light bread and churned about four pounds of butter. All of this was still setting on the table by which Jonas very quickly seated himself. I began to cut him some meat, but he took the whole chunk, also all the rest of the fixed food on the table, and put all in his sack and rushed out.

In about an hour my folks came back from the barn. My brother, sister and I had hidden beneath the table, for we were afraid the folks would scold us for the food all being gone. They saw what had happened and asked the cause. I told them what happened and they never scolded us.

The next morning Dad went into Dupree. It was then that everyone that Jonas had visited the night before told the same story. Several years later when we had known more of the Indians, they told us that Jonas had done the same trick amongst his own people about the same night. One of the young Sioux happened to be at Owl King's home when Jonas returned with his loot the next day and that he had two large sacks full of food. Jonas never married. His should-be wife was his brother Albert's wife, Mabel.

Another time Jonas made up his mind he wanted a white school teacher for his own. There was a school teacher's homestead just south of my Dad's place. This teacher became a close friend of Mother's so she would tell Mother a lot of her troubles.

One night when there was no moon, this teacher said she heard a noise outside towards her coal shed so she got her gun and opened the house door. Her dog jumped out in front of her and raced on towards where the noise came from. The teacher flashed her light, a kerosene lantern, on an object that looks like a big bear crawling on all fours. She shot but her aim was too high and she hit her coal shed. The object raised up and it is Jonas Owl King. She asked Jonas what he wanted and in his broken English he tells her that he, Jonas, wanted a white wife and he aimed to stay all night in her shed and come get her in the morning. The teacher made her threats and sends Jonas off faster than he came.

At our new home we have many Indian families for our neighbors. Several of their children go to school with us. Mr. Edward Swan had two girls. Mr. Dick Swan had a boy and a girl. Mr. Oscar Bridwell had two girls and two boys. Then in between there was Mr. Philip Brownwolf, but their children all went to school at Pierre Indian Boarding School. When school was out in the spring there were several young people home from different schools. It was one of these young men who in 1922 became my husband.

That was a queer meeting for two young people. In August or September, I just don't recall, there was a big fair and rodeo going on at Faith. Mr. Brownwolf's family had all gone and left their son, John, home alone. He was going later on horseback. He had been going by our place before and he would stop and talk to all, whomever he saw. Well this one time he decided that maybe we could go with him to the fair. He loaded his record player into the buggy drawn by two horses and he came over to Dad, and asked Dad, "Mr. Lee, I would like to trade my record player for your girl." Of course Dad did not approve but after he left I did a lot of coaxing and wanted to go to the fair, so Dad said I could go with the Bridwell girls to the fair, so I went. I came home about four days later, and John bringing me. Dad asked him to take his record player home so it wouldn't get broken. John said, "No, I traded for your girl." So we were married December 29, 1922 in Dupree by Rev. Owens. Avie Langor, Geecy and Thomas Kills First were our witnesses. Born to this young couple were five children.

Let's go a few years again and enjoy a laugh when Grandma was a young girl. Sometime either in May before school in the fall, I with my parents were living with an aunt and uncle who had four children, two of them school age. Course there was no school close to home in those days. See this happened around 1909, in the southern part of Missouri. Well, anyway as all young kids, I wanted to go to school with my cousins. After several times begging my parents to go to school, they finally gave their consent. So off to school we three girls walked. It seemed a long way. Things went smoothly at school and time to go home finally came around. On the way to school we had to cross a brook on step stones. We got to this brook on the way home. Our mothers were calling to us to hurry up because there was a storm coming up close. "Don't play in the brook," they were saying. But not heeding our mothers' warnings, we stopped, took off our shoes and hose and waded in the brook. Mother kept calling to me that there were tortoises in the brook and they were called snapping turtles. If one got hold of one of my toes it would not let go until it thundered. But still we waded in the brook. All at once I remembered! I screamed, "Help me, Cousin Mary. A turtle has hold of my toe." But the other two had left me with my big toe in the turtle's mouth. Then, all at once a large clap of thunder came. Lo and behold, the turtle did let go my toe and took off down the stream. I got out of the brook in a hurry and went on home. I lost my big toenail as a result.

Then again my folks moved to northern Missouri where another Uncle and Aunt lived. Nothing would do but to go and stay with this Aunt out in the country. So my folks took me out there. Auntie had lots of chickens and the hens would hide their nests everywhere in the mangers out in the barn where there was always a white mare tied in a stall. Auntie always told 'em "Be careful of the horse when you gather eggs. She might bite you." On this special evening I forgot the horse in the barn and went in front of her along the manger where there was a nest full of eggs. This old horse grabbed me on the back of the neck. If I hadn't had on a large sunbonnet, the horse would have hurt my neck real bad, but it didn't go through the cloth.

Then early in October 1909, I was to go to the county fair with this same Aunt. She told me I had to speak a piece in front of the crowd. I was very scared but I learned, "Twinkle, Twinkle, Little Star." When the time came for me to go to the center, I crawled beneath my Aunt's skirt. The man who was looking for me saw where I was hiding and he got hold of me and carried me to the middle of the crowd, stood me up on top of a hundred-gallon vinegar barrel. After some pleading, I finally spoke my little poem. When I was through, this man gave me a blue glass bead necklace.

In 1911, after my folks had built a few houses out of sod, such as chicken houses, we were bothered with bull snakes robbing the hens' nests and coyotes digging into chicken houses and eating chickens. On this certain night my mother told me, "There must be a coyote out in the chicken house." There was such a noise! She wanted me to go with her and carry the lantern. I was very scared but went anyway. Mother opened the hen house door. Lo and behold, there was a coyote eating a hen. Mother told me to stay in the door way and she would go and kill this coyote. She had a small ax in her hand so she made a pass at the coyote but out the door it goes—right between my legs. Oh, how I screamed, but that did no good.

[This story was never finished because Mother had arthritis and just couldn't write anymore.]

# Sarah Campbell
## Lawrence County
## 1874

The tall grass in the abandoned cemetery of ghost-like Galena nearly obscures the grave of the first woman, (excepting Sioux [women]), to enter the Black Hills. This title has long been bestowed on Mrs. Annie Tallent, but actually history shows that it belongs to "Aunt Sally." Mrs. Tallent would more accurately be described as the "first white woman" to enter the Black Hills because "Aunt Sally" was a Negro.

Proof that "Aunt Sally" was in the Black Hills several months before Mrs. Tallent is contained in the official report of the Custer expedition to the Hills of 1874. The famous frontier cavalry officer, General George A. Custer, was placed in command of the expedition charged with investigating rumors of gold in the Black Hills in 1874. The expedition consisted of 10 companies of the Seventh Cavalry, one each of the 17th and 20th Infantries, a detachment of 100 Indian scouts, together with the necessary guides, interpreters and teamsters, two practical miners, several engineers, geologists, a naturalist, botanist, medical officers, a photographer and several newspapermen. There were about 1,000 men altogether in the expedition and one lone woman—"Aunt Sally." The wagon train consisted of 110 wagons, each drawn by six mules, and ambulances. There were also 1,000 cavalry horses and 300 beeves for slaughter as food along the way. The expedition was described as the best equipped for service on the plains in the history of the U.S. Army.

The expedition left Fort Lincoln at Bismarck, on July 2, 1874, and 28 days later it was in the scenic valley where Custer, the "Mother City" of the Black Hills, is now located. It was here that Horatio N. Ross, one of the practical miners in the party, made his historic gold find on French Creek on July 30, 1874.

The gold discovery eventually led to the hurried settlement of the Black Hills — and the death of Custer and 274
men of the Seventh Cavalry on the Little Big Horn in Mon-
tana two years later. Custer named the valley where gold
had been discovered "Golden Valley" and his dispatches about
it brought on the illegal settlement of the region. But the
resentful Sioux obtained their revenge on Custer by ending
his colorful career and wiping out his entire command in
the Battle of the Little Big Horn.

The first official mention of "Aunt Sally" is contained
in a report of establishment of the first mining company
in the Black Hills. The company was formed on Aug. 5,
1874, only five days after Ross made the initial discovery,
and the formation was reported by Correspondent William
E. Curtis of the Chicago Tribune.

Correspondent Curtis ended his dispatch by stating, "Thus
were made insignificantly and illegally, perhaps, the inci-
pient efforts toward the development of one of the most
rich and beautiful pieces of Nature's embroidery on God's
footstool."

Curtis reported that the company was organized on
French Creek, two and a half miles below the present town
of Custer, when a meeting was held around a camp fire among
a cluster of wagons. The company was formed according
to the laws of the United States and the territory of Dakota
with authorized officers and board of directors.

The founders posted the following notice on the inside
of a hard tack box cover and placed it on the claim: "District
No. 1 Custer Park Mining Company, Custer's Gulch, Black
Hills, D.T., August 5, 1874 — Notice is hereby given that
we the undersigned claimants do claim 4,000 feet commenc-
ing at No. 8 above, and running down to No. 12 below
Discovery, for mining purposes, and intend to work the same
as soon as peaceable possession can be had of this portion
of Dakota Territory by the general government, and we do
hereby locate the above claim in accordance with the laws
of Dakota Territory governing mining districts."

There follows the names of 12 claimants for locations
below the Discovery claim, and eight claimants for locations
below Discovery.

Listed on the historic document as claiming No. 7 below Discovery is the name of Sarah Campbell. Freeman Steele of Sturgis, life-time resident of the Black Hills and a member of the Society of Black Hills Pioneers, said he first learned about "Aunt Sally" from two members of the 1874 Custer expedition. Steele disclosed that the late Dan Newell of Sturgis and the late Charles Windolph of Lead told him about "Aunt Sally's" part in the Custer expedition. They claimed that she was a cook for Capt. Keogh, one of the Seventh Cavalry officers in the expedition, who was later killed along with Custer in the Battle of the Little Big Horn.

"Newell and Windolph told me that 'Aunt Solly,' as they called her, was brought along on the expedition by Capt. Keogh. It had to be a man of rank to get permission for a woman to go along on such an expedition. Capt. Keogh, a southerner, was a man of means aside from his Army pay and he obtained 'Aunt Sally' when the regiment was stationed in the South some years earlier."

"Keogh preferred the colored woman's 'beating biscuits' to the Army food," Steele explained, "and he was wealthy enough to afford the expense of a private cook. Newell and Windolph told me many times that Aunt Sally was a highly respected woman and she would use her frying pan on any trooper who got fresh with her."

Steele said many persons have claimed to have served with Custer in the 1874 expedition, and Newell and Windolph would test these claimants by asking, "Who was the woman in the expedition?" "If the answer was 'Aunt Sally,' the two oldtimers would agree that the man knew what he was talking about," Steele added. "But if he didn't know the answer, he would be branded as a hoaxster. Everybody in that expedition knew Aunt Sally!"

History has failed to record much of what happened to "Aunt Sally" after the Custer expedition left the Black Hills. The Custer County records still contain her claim to No. 7 below Discovery, but it is not known whether she ever returned to work the claim.

Shortly after the Custer expedition left the Hills, the Collins-Russell party entered it. This party included Mrs. Annie Tallent as the one woman in the expedition and it arrived on the Custer campsite in "Golden Valley" on Dec.

23, 1874. The Collins-Russell party, however, was chased out of the Hills by U.S. troops and Mrs. Tallent went to Cheyenne, Wyoming. She returned to the area the following year and later became the first superintendent of schools in Pennington County.

The last mention of this curious frontier character is contained in the April 13, 1888, edition of the *Black Hills Daily Times,* the early-day Deadwood newspaper. It states, briefly:

"Undertaker Smith was called to Galena yesterday to assist in the interment of 'Old Aunt Sally,' a colored woman, aged 75 years, who died of general debility at her ranch four miles from Galena Tuesday. Aunt Sally was a well-known character; she claimed to have been the first woman to enter the Hills, arriving in 1874 as cook for General Custer. She returned in 1876 and for a short time lived at Crook. Later she moved to near Galena and located on the ranch where she died. She was well known by all oldtimers and was universally respected."

# "Mother and Dakota"
## Mary Ellen Cleaver Clark
## Aurora County
## 1883

### by her son, Badger Clark

*[In 1883 the family moved to Dakota Territory and took up a homestead four miles south of Plankinton, where they lived until 1887, when they moved to Mitchell. In 1893, they moved to Huron and in 1898 to Deadwood, where Mrs. Clark died in the same year.]*

Father built a church in Ottumwa in the early eighties and got too enthusiastic about it. Apparently he labored under that delusion so common among business and professional men of today, the human-dynamo complex, and forgot that his body was mortal. He realized his mistake when the doctors told him that he could remain a citizen of this world only if he dropped preaching and all the nerve-straining activities of his profession and took up outdoor work, not too heavy, for the rest of his life.

About that time the railroads were building into Dakota Territory and "opening it up." Father's brother, a lawyer, had already contracted the free-land fever and taken up a homestead, writing letters back to father full of Dakota-pioneer optimism, so our family turned their faces Dakotaward. To all but father the change was welcome. Mother had lived on a Pennsylvania farm in her girlhood, and looked forward happily to fresh air and freedom. Hal, my eldest brother, then fourteen, said, "Goody! I've always wanted to go out in the woods and chop down a great big tree." Poor Hal! His new home turned out to be a spot where there wasn't a tree within twenty miles.

So it came to pass that the family settled on a quarter-section four miles south of Plankinton in April, '83. They picked a homesite on the highest point in the tract, as Dakota farmers always have—to get the full benefit of the wind, apparently—and fell to work building a house. It was quite an imposing house on the outside, and it was a story and a half, but the insulation was defective as father did not have enough money to plaster it. However, it kept out the rain and part of the wind and sheltered us and our household goods, and the bright particular jewel of the latter being a reed organ on which mother was teaching herself to play in her scanty leisure hours. There was no well, nor money to dig one, so our water for the house had to be hauled three miles in barrels. Luckily there was a slough in the pasture which took care of the stock.

As to my account of those years and more on the Aurora County Farm, I must acknowledge that it is hearsay evidence, for at the time of our coming from Iowa I had barely attained the interesting age of three months.

I have always regretted that I could not have seen my mother when she was young. I was her last child and she was forty when I was born, so I knew her only in middle age. I remember hair of so deep a brown that at first glance one would call it black, and rather large blue eyes. One evening when I was about eight years old, I amused myself by making a sketch of her face in profile, when we talked and her busy hands knitted. Of course it was not a good likeness, but it fixed her features firmly in my memory. I remember especially the good-natured little crinkles about her eyes which my awkward pencil could not reproduce.

The only descriptions I ever had of her youthful appearance came from dad, and he, I'm afraid, was a prejudiced witness. He used to tell of his first sight of her. He had been invalided home from the Union army, and was riding through Mount Pleasant when he beheld her, standing on a corner and waiting to cross the muddy street. "And instantly, I said to myself, 'I'll marry that girl if she's marriageable.' " She also noticed him in that fateful moment but, according to her laughing account, her first impression was quite different. As she saw him, heavily bearded, slumped over on his horse by the weakness of his wartime disabilities and still dressed in his faded blue uniform, she took him for a graybeard—the Graybeards being a regiment of home guards recruited among men too old for field service.

Nevertheless, as his health improved and he took up the work of a Methodist Circuit rider, he managed an introduction to her and they were soon engaged. I still have their love letters, written during the year before their marriage. One night he had a date with her—in modern parlance—but received word in the afternoon that some unexpected duty would call him out of town on the evening train, so on his way to the station, he stopped at her mother's house to make his excuses and say goodbye. It was a summer night and she was sitting on the sill of an open window, enjoying the moon. When he left her it was quite natural that she should lean out of the window and kiss him. The little letter she wrote him later that night, when she realized the awful thing she had done, and her terror lest some passer-by had noted their Romeo and Juliet performance in the brilliant moonlight, would be very amusing to the young folks of today.

In 1912, my father went back to the fiftieth anniversary of his regiment in Mount Pleasant, and I went with him. The old house of my grandmother was still standing at that time and dad pointed out to me the very window where mother had committed her dreadful indiscretion half a century before.

Father always had a deep appreciation—a decorous and proper appreciation—of feminine beauty. He was very frank about it and in my boyhood, when he praised some woman's good looks, he amused mother by invariably saying, "she has a fine eye." So I conclude that in her youth my mother must have had a particularly fine eye.

She always had an eye for beauty in nature, at any rate. The pristine freshness of the prairies delighted her, and she often told me of those first days on the claim. The incredible richness of the waving grasses, grasses which had never been mowed except by the buffalo herds whose wallows still pitted the prairie, the sunrises and sunsets and the wide glory of the sky, the "boom! boom! boom!" of the courting prim prairie chickens, the melodies of the meadow larks and all the weird, wild cry of the plovers—all these and the utter newness and cleanness of the whole country gave her a feeling of beginning life over again in her forties.

The boys were young and father was able to do little
in the first year, so she had the management of the farm—
and me—on her hands, but she was equal to it. Father had
been apprenticed a carpenter in his teens and liked the work,
so he attended to the building operations, doing as much
as he could himself, but she was the farmer. With me on
her hip some of the time, she supervised the sod breaking
and the fence building; she taught Hal to milk and did part
of it herself, and on occasions she even pitched hay. The
first crop of wheat brought the thrashers with their horse-
power machine and hurried huge cooking jobs in the house,
with the kindly help of neighbor women but mighty slim
facilities, and at mealtimes the jam of dusty, sweaty men.
How much the folks made out of that crop and the ones
that-followed I don't know, but it couldn't have been much.
I do know that, like all Dakota pioneers, they acquired, along
with other new possessions, an incubus called the Mortgage.
As I grew and began to try to understand things, years
after, I had an impression that The Mortgage was an un-
wieldy animal, like an elephant, which was very expensive
to feed. I learned better in time, but the Mortgage was an
unloved member of our household for years and years.

Hardships? Oh yes, of course. But the hardships were
expected as a part of pioneer life, and the pioneers felt a
certain pride in the way they took them and lived through.
All the pioneers I've known seemed to make less fuss about
real trials and tribulations than moderns do about small
physical discomforts and inconveniences. The winters were
bitter and the summers were hot. If they were not colder
and hotter than those at present, the lack of defenses against
extremes of temperature made them seem so. And the lux-
uriant grass made frightening prairie fires. Once in the fall
father and the boys were out with the neighbors fighting
a fire, when a change of wind brought the flames leaping
toward our home, where mother and I were alone. The garden,
on the side of the house next to the fire, was a mass of
dry weeds, so mother, propping me up where she could keep
an eye on me through the smoke, harnessed an old horse
to a light plow and proceeded to tear up the garden as a
firebreak as best she could, while I, no doubt, howled an
accompaniment to her labors. The menfolks at a distance

saw the direction the fire was taking and came home at a gallop across the blackened prairie, followed by others, so the farmstead was saved. That was a great day in mother's memory. I know by the way that she told me the story that there was a great thrill, mingled with her fright.

Of course I had no share in pioneer hardships. I was cuddled in love and soft flannel and fed on pure cream from our several cows and, as mother told me later, grew so fat that I could hardly open my eyes. A "formula" might have been better, but I seem to have done very well on what I had. When I was two, as mother told me, I could manage a fair "second" to certain hymn tunes that the family sang with the organ. I don't recall that. In fact, the only sharp memories I have of those first years on the farm are my terror of the whirring, roaring, banging thrashing machine, and the thrilling adventure of being chased by a turkey gobbler that didn't approve of my pink sunbonnet.

In two years the farm restored my father to robust health, however unkind it may have been to him financially, and he began dreaming to be back to his first love, preaching. He was asked to conduct services at this or that schoolhouse and to fill temporarily vacant pulpits in this or that town church. He was no farmer and he knew it, but in the pulpit he "had liberty", as he expressed it, and so, after three years and more on the farm, he was offered the pastorate at Mitchell and gladly accepted. Mother made no objection. Back in his circuit-riding days, when he was courting her, he had written her of the joy of "standing on the walls of Zion" and she, in reply, had acknowledged a modest desire to stand there with him, and that was just what she did to the end of her life.

In Mitchell, mother took up my religious education seriously. I was taught to repeat "Now I lay me" at her knee in the old fashion, so early that I don't know just when it began. Next came "Our Father," which I associate with mastering the art of dressing and undressing myself without help, for they came about the same time. I knelt at my bed with mother beside me, and she dictated that supreme prayer a few words at a time until it was fixed in my mind and I could manage alone. This gave me personally, quite a sense of achievement. Being able to say my prayers and to go to bed all by myself, I felt that I was almost on the verge of maturity.

Later, when I began to read, I was given a simply-worded story of the Bible which I went through several times. We always had family prayers in the morning and there I learned to love the King James version, whose rolling cadences fitted my father's mellow bass voice perfectly. Nowadays, I am sometimes stunned to find university students with only a vague and garbled knowledge of the Bible, and some with virtually none at all. All the college degrees in the alphabet can't make a fully educated person without a knowledge of that cornerstone of our culture, the Bible.

It was shortly after we came to Mitchell that I got my first full-length memory portrait of my mother. She had made a new dress, perhaps the first really dressy dress she had had for three years. It was of a soft gray woolen material — I can see the subdued pattern of it yet — and she came out of the bedroom in it to undergo inspection. There she stands in the lamplight, smoothing down the skirt with her hands, a little shy under dad's scrutiny and enthusiastic approval.

Another flashback to early Mitchell days — a blizzardy night, and dad, who has come to town on a late Milwaukee freight train, thundering on the storm door at three o'clock in the morning. Mother, in her nightdress, opens the door and he comes in like a polar bear, his fur cap and buffalo overcoat all driven full of snow. "Have you heard about the college?" "No, what has happened?" "It's burned to the ground!" And so it was. The brand-new first building of Dakota Wesleyan, which father and his fellow Methodists had planned for and begged for and prayed for and worried over for so long, was a smoking ruin, with one student dead and several maimed.

Another flashback — the blizzard of '88. The swirling, hissing chaos of snow that wiped out the world so suddenly on that warm, cloudy January morning. My brothers, one at the post office and the other at college, not trying to come home that day or night. The long afternoon when dad and Brother Washburn, an old ministerial friend who is visiting us, take turns reading from a novel by E. P. Roe, pitching their voices high to get above the endless roar of the wind. The next morning, beautiful under a brilliant sun,

with snowdrifts like sculptured marble, the boys arriving
early with cheeks red from the cold and a jolly breakfast.

We went back and spent a summer on the farm when
I was seven years old. We had our usual farming luck, for
that was a summer of the hot winds. People said they came
from Kansas, which gave me a prejudice against Kansas
I was years getting over. One morning we had forty acres
of green and promising corn; in the evening the seared leaves
rustled stiffly in the wind and our corn crop had gone the
way of so many farmer's dreams.

Early in the summer there was a bright spot for my
mother, when my brother Fred, seventeen years old and a
mere college prep, won the state intercollegiate oratorical
contest. There was a grand reception for him at the college
and we drove down. Behold my brother in a borrowed silk
tie, a borrowed cutaway coat and a borrowed gold-headed
cane. And a pair of scholarly-looking nose glasses with gold
frames which he didn't need at all but wore "for style" and
to make him look older. Fred was painfully conscious of
his youth. I gazed at him with awe and was flattered when
he spoke to me, though his fraternal greeting was limited
to "Hello Sprout."

Nowadays the Fourth of July is safe and sane – and dull,
a holiday like other holidays. But then it was a special day
for boys, gorgeous with explosives and excitement. That year
some Yankee had invented a machine to make firecrackers
in this country, instead of importing them from China. They
were colored a patriotic red, white and blue, rather than
the common Chinese red, and were a handsome product, but
they had one fault – four-fifths of them failed to go off. The
Fourth on the farm, mother thought she would give my day
a joyous beginning by awakening me with firecrackers, so
she placed half a bunch under an old dishpan beneath my
window, lighted the fuse and retired to a safe distance. But
nothing happened except a drift of smoke from under the
dishpan and a few fizzles. She tried again with the same
result, and finally had to come in and wake me in the ordinary way. She was so disappointed over the failure of her
kindly little surprise that for the first time in my life I didn't
take my mother and her doings for granted. I felt sorry
for her and tried to please her by appearing very happy

all day, though there was not much fun to be had out of those inert firecrackers.

I never saw our farm again after that summer. A few years later, when it was unoccupied, a tornado dipped down and scattered house, barn and sheds all over a couple of sections and they were never rebuilt. Nothing survived but The Mortgage.

Those were pioneer days in town as well as in the country, and the amenities of living in Mitchell were not much superior to those on the farm. Mother's household water system, for instance, consisted of a pump at the back door, with a full tub under it where we watered our buggy horse, old Fan. One day when I was about nine years old, a neighbor boy and I got into a box of old clothes in the barn and conceived the idea of giving an elaborately costumed minstrel show. Mother was down town at a church sale that Saturday afternoon, so Fred and I had a free hand. There was a whirlwind advertising campaign in the neighborhood, and soon ten or a dozen boys and girls climbed the ladder into our haymow, admission ten pins each. Our program was wholly ad lib. We dressed ourselves as our wild fancy dictated and blacked our faces with soot from an old joint of stovepipe, doing it very thoroughly and paying particular attention to the ears and back of the neck.

I suppose the high point in the show was sort of a war dance which Fred did solo, dressed in a skirt he had fashioned out of an old stiff-bosomed shirt of dad's. I was behind the screen, pulling on an old pair of boots preparatory to my turn when Fred, with a froglike leap, landed on top of me. He was much in need of privacy, as his skirt had dropped off. Mother got home as Fred and I were trying to wash off our soot at the tub under the pump — in cold water and without soap. Mildly alarmed by our appearance at first, her mood changed quickly when we told her about our show and asked advice as to getting the soot off. It is good to remember a mother's prayers, and it is also good to remember her laughter. When we found that no reprimand was forthcoming, Fred and I joined in her merriment and giggled consumedly.

Today, home seems to be a place to get away from as much as possible. Women loudly complain of its monotony;

men are expected to grab every chance to go to lodge in the evening or sit in at a poker game; children must be provided with expensive downtown recreation centers to keep them out of worse places. But in my boyhood we spent our evenings at home by preference. There was an occasional church doings or lecture or concert, and we enjoyed them, but home was always best.

What a boy home I had! Those winter evenings, the soft light of the kerosene lamp, the base-burner stove with its abundant isinglass and its hard-coal fire glowing like a great jewel, and we! The boys were in college and of dating age, so they were often absent, but father and mother and I held the fort. Father loved to read aloud and we loved to have him. Dickens, Victor Hugo, Lew Wallace, Tom Moore's *Lalla Rookh*, Tennyson's *Idylls of the King*—how we adventured with the heroes and heroines all over the world! After a couple of hours of reading, dad would get up and pace the floor to stretch his legs. He would assume the part of the hero in the current story and address mother with the name of the heroine, apostrophizing her as his queen, his sultana, his full moon of full moons, his rose of the world, while mother and I laughed at his histrionics. Then we would have some popcorn or some apples from the barrel in the cellar before we went to bed.

They were an odd pair, those two. By the time I was old enough to notice things they had been married fully twenty-five years, yet sometimes when I was alone with them I felt almost like a crowd. One night I remember when we were driving across the prairie under a full moon, they on the buggy seat and I on a little box at their feet, they sang "Roll on, silver moon, guide the traveler on his way" in a manner which, as I look back on it, had much of the glamour of young love.

Mother was something of a pioneer in ideas. For one thing, she refused to wear a corset, a procedure in those days eccentric to the verge of impropriety. I liked it, for when I hugged her alone, in a spasm of affection—or when I was teasing for something—she felt human and alive, while other ladies, if I happened accidentally to touch them at the waistline, felt like telegraph poles. Mother had a very neat figure in middle age and she was probably aware of it, though the stern Quaker training of her girlhood forbade her to reveal any such worldly vanity.

She was also a person of advanced ideas in her support of woman suffrage, a position which was not considered quite ladylike at the time. She took a warm interest in politics and argued that if women could vote everything would be better. She never spoke in public on that or any other subject – she left all that sort of thing to the other side of the house – but if the matter came up in private conversation, nobody was left in the dark as to her sentiments. Once when I was very young, I went with the folks to hear Susan B. Anthony, but I have only a dim recollection of the elderly lady in black who strode back and forth on the stage of the old opera house, speaking vehemently. Father laughed for years afterward over the vicious emphasis with which Susan said "the MEN." Susan didn't have much use for them.

And of course mother stood for temperance, or rather total abstinence. About the only time I recall her flaming into really hot wrath was one week when she befriended the pathetic wife of a drunkard. Those were days of great hopes and dreams. They even dreamed and hoped that in twenty years or so the "curse of rum" would be lifted forever from our country. I am glad mother did not live to see women – mothers – quite at home in the saloon, and ladies at social gatherings glass in hand, with unnaturally bright eyes and unnaturally loose tongues. Among my other obsolete sentiments is a fervent gratitude that in my childhood my mother never kissed me good night, with her breath smelling like a distillery.

Some time after we moved to Huron in '93, my brother Fred died of tuberculosis at the age of twenty-one, after nearly four years of decline. Had the doctors known as much then, as they do now, he might still be alive, but in those days there was little to do but watch him die. He was easily the brightest of the family and his passing was a heavy grief to the folks. Mother had nursed him, of course, and at that time, we did not fully realize that the disease was transmissible. Her usually robust health slowly failed after that and there came a winter when she could no longer work, and we got our first maid.

Mother was still able to be up all day, and that winter she beguiled the time by taking painting lessons from a woman in the next block who was proficient in that line. For months, at her easel in the living room, she found new delights in color and form as she painted from "studies." I have two of her pictures hanging here in the cabin now, not masterpieces by any means but treasures to me because I watched so many of the brush strokes and knew so well the hand that laid them on.

As she went steadily downhill and the doctors could do little but shake their heads, father seized an opportunity to transfer to Deadwood in 1898, in the hope that the change of climate and altitude might benefit her. It was a vain hope, and she left us that fall.

One morning during her last days here, she called me into her room. At the age of fifteen death was an unreal thing to me, but that morning, as I saw the thinness of her face in which the blue eyes seemed to shine more blue than ever, my heart suddenly sank and I knew I was going to lose her. I sat down on the edge of the bed and she reached out and took my hand.

"I had a strange dream last night," she said. "I was going to tell your father, but he has many things to worry about now, so I'll tell you and you can tell him—afterward. I dreamed I was walking through a thick, dark forest. The trail was rough with rocks and fallen logs, and I often caught my foot and stumbled in the dimness, but these things did not worry me so much as the thought that somewhere ahead lay the Great River of Death. You know, I have always been timid about water and I had heard that this river had neither bridge nor ferry, yet in some way I would have to cross it."

"As I went along, a little stream of black water ran across the trail—not muddy water but black, like ink. I stepped over it easily and might not have noticed it except for the strange look of the water. From there on the trees thinned out and the sunlight broke through and presently I reached the edge of the forest, where the trail, smooth and firm now, wound away through a sunny meadow with many flowers among the grass. A man was coming toward me on the trail and his face was so kind that I was not afraid to speak to him, and I said: 'Can you tell me how far it is to the Great River of Death?' And he smiled at me and answered: 'Do you remember the little black stream you stepped across, back there in the shadows? That was the River of Death.' "

And so, two days afterward, mother stepped easily across the little black rill of her dream and went pioneering into the most wonderful new country of all.

# La Vicie Marie Kale George
# Potter County
# 1889

La Vicie Marie Kale George came to Gettysburg January 9, 1889, at the age of 17. She came to South Dakota with her brother-in-law on the train through Hawarden, Iowa, where they changed cars and came on to Gettysburg.

There they were met by the brother-in-law's brother, who took them to Mrs. O'Brien's hotel to get warm, after which they got in a sled with a team hitched to it and started off to the brother-in-law's and sister's home which was a mile and a half west of Agar.

La Vicie helped by hauling water from a well near Okobojie Creek two and a half miles away and did other chores until the first of March, 1890, at which time the brother-in-law and sister loaded up their belongings in a wagon and moved to Mitchell, leaving La Vicie there in an empty house. They thought by doing so to force her to marry the brother-in-law's brother and live with him on his claim across the road.

La Vicie had no idea of marriage and told the brother that if he had a spark of manhood he would take her to Gettysburg. He agreed to take her there, if she would bake him some bread. He furnished the ingredients for the bread, and La Vicie rigged up an old stove that was left in the shed, gathered up cow chips to burn in it, and baked it. She stayed all night alone in the empty house sleeping on the floor, and all the cover she had was her coat.

After the bread was baked, he took her to Gettysburg. Now La Vicie didn't know a soul in Gettysburg. She knew a teacher that taught the school her sister's little girl went to, and the teacher's people lived in Gettysburg, or about a mile south of Gettysburg. The man dumped her off at their place, and she knocked at the door and asked if she could stay there all night. The dear old mother said: "You bet you can" and gave her a hearty welcome. She browned some wheat and other grains and made coffee, grinding them up in a coffee mill.

The next day La Vicie walked to Gettysburg and got a job washing dishes in the National Hotel. Here she obtained her room and board. In two weeks she was promoted to dining room work, and after two or three weeks of that she was advanced to chamber room work. After doing that a short while she thought she would take up her trade of dress making and sew for the hotel help. She made arrangements with a couple of milliners, Mrs. Berdick and Mrs. Ellis, to use their sewing machine until she made enough money to buy one of her own.

She soon bought an old machine from a Mrs. Liablin, which was so gummed up and rusty that both she and Mrs. Liablin could not by combined effort make run. However, she took it to town after paying $10.00 for it, and took it all apart, scraping, polishing and oiling it, after which it would sew anything from a tug of harness to a veil. It was a White machine, and while it sewed well, it sounded like a threshing machine. After she was married, and as soon as her husband could find the money, he bought her a new one.

She had plenty of business. She made dresses for $1.00 apiece. She made silk dresses and wedding dresses, and even today many tell her that she made their wedding dress. She went out to sew by the day or week; Mrs. Colby in Lebanon for two weeks, Mrs. Hinckley north of town for three weeks, etc. Finally she rented a room in a family home and took her machine there and did dress making and tailoring for the stores in town.

Several times in the early days there were Indian scares, and the men would gather all their weapons together and make ready to protect the settlement. People from the country would come to town and bring what they could with them, sometimes a featherbed on the back of a cow, etc. Once a company of cavalry was stationed there for about three months, expecting an attack.

Brooks George was the clerk in the National Hotel where La Vicie worked first, and he took an extra fancy to her. He looked so young that when he asked her to go to a party with him, she said she wouldn't go out with a boy, but he convinced her that he was older than she. From then on he never let her go anywhere alone, and after two years of courtship they were married.

At the time they were married, Brooks worked for Mr. F. D. Teall in a general store, for $25.00 a month. After seven years, Mr. J. B. Clark, a farmer, bought the store from Mr. Teall, and the bargain included Brooks George to run it. For eight more years he managed the store for Mr. Clark, with very little increase in salary. When Mr. Clark took his son-in-law in as partner, Brooks thought it was time he got out and devoted his efforts to running a store for himself, so he did just that. He successfully ran his own business from that time to 1947, when he passed on.

La Vicie went to New York for golden brown taffeta silk for her wedding dress, and made it herself. It is still a wonderful dress, the material still looks like new, after being worn many times in 61 years. It has a floor length skirt with a basque waist and passementerie trimming. La Vicie, still slim and straight, wore it on her golden wedding day in 1941.

One of the wedding dresses that La Vicie made was for a bride that came over from Germany to marry an unknown groom. La Vicie was invited to the wedding and asked to help dress the bride. The wedding was held in a country school house near the house where the family lived, and the bride walked through the stubblefield to the school house, letting her veil blow in the wind and it was badly snagged on the stubble. It didn't bother her. During the wedding celebration they had much beer and dancing, and her whole costume would not survive more than one wedding. La Vicie found herself dancing, clasped to the bosom of a fat old German lady, who swung her off her feet and round and round until she was dizzy. They whirled until the fat lady became tired. Soon her steady beau Brooks came and took her home.

Picnics were the chief form of recreation in summer, and one that La Vicie never will forget was the first one she attended. It was held on the Forest City river banks. They had begun to build the railroad to Forest City and there were high grades that were crossed by the wagon roads. That 4th of July it was so cold that La Vicie wore her plush coat to keep warm. Going over one of those high grades the broncos hitched to the rig became frightened and dashed over the grade into a big pond on the other side, throwing everybody out of the rig except La Vicie's date for that day, the aforementioned brother-in-law's brother. Trying to catch himself he spread his arms and legs and looked just like a huge bullfrog as he fell out of the rig on his back into the muddy water.

Although they were all shaken and bruised, La Vicie thought it was the funniest thing she had ever seen and laughed and laughed. What made it funnier was that nobody else saw anything humorous about it and became quite indignant that she could laugh in the face of such a catastrophe. No one was seriously hurt.

After La Vicie and Brooks were married, father George loaned them a cow to milk, and said they could buy a calf and raise their own cow. La Vicie bought a good sized calf from the butcher, and then Brooks bought a calf from the country. La Vicie's calf was gentle but Brook's calf was wild and hard to handle. Before they got rid of it, it bunted La Vicie when she went to feed it and brought on her seven months baby. La Vicie was in critical condition for a long time, but the baby lived and is her only daughter who is still living. There were no incubators for tiny babies in those days, and it was only by the tenderest care that she survived.

While La Vicie was critically ill in bed, one of the rare South Dakota cyclones occurred. The storm blew a big beam from a building that was wrecked near them through the window of the room where La Vicie was. Brooks held a quilt up to the window to protect La Vicie and she expected to see another beam come and kill him any minute.

During that year Father George became very ill and was brought from the farm to their little home. He had an abscess on his lung caused by injuries in the Civil War. They had a doctor come from Huron, but the doctors were unskilled and inexperienced in those days, and they didn't know what to do for him, so he passed away.

After that the young couple had mother George and her younger son William to look after. They did what they could to help William get his education. With what help they could give him, and his own efforts, he studied to be a doctor, and at this time is one of the state's oldest doctors.

Finding a place to live was as hard is those days as it is at the present time. There were just not very many houses, and pioneers kept moving in. After cleaning and decorating several places which would be sold and they would have to look for another, they moved into a big old barn of a place which was called the Buffalo House. It was the first house of any size in Gettysburg and had housed many people. One of the trees in town was a big old cottonwood in front of the Buffalo House.

Brooks and La Vicie decided to build their own home, and picked a site across the street from the Buffalo House, where they built a little two room house. It was clean and new and snug.

The time came when Mother George had to come to live with them so they moved the little house to the other end of the street and built on more rooms. The town has built up around it, so that now it is in the center of town.

While the house was being remodeled, La Vicie was expecting another child. One day she was standing at the window watching her little daughter go to school, and she saw a runaway team of horses come around the corner, and it appeared they caught on a wagon which stood in the street and one of the horses seemed to fall right on the little girl. A man picked her up with head over one arm and heels over the other and started home with her. La Vicie threw a shawl around her and started to meet them, expecting the child was crushed, but as she approached the man the child raised her head and said: "I'm all right, mama." The blood gushed from her nose and throat as she spoke, and scared La Vicie even more.

It happened, however, that a miracle had occurred. The child had seen the team coming, started to jump over the wagon tongue, and fell underneath it. The horse fell on top of it, and the wagon tongue held, so the child was only scratched and shocked from the experience.

Soon after this a son was born to them. With the kind of care confinement cases got in those days, La Vicie nearly died at this birth also. She was never well until she went to the hospital at Aberdeen and had a complete overhaul job. But the son was a fine, healthy child and grew up to be a source of comfort and pride.

La Vicie's life has been very active and useful. She is now past 80 and lives alone in a house that was enlarged to ten rooms in the closing year of the First World War. She takes care of her own business, drives her own car, taking her friends many places with her, and still is active in the Literary Club and Eastern Star. She has been a member of the Literary Club for 36 years, and the Eastern Star since 1923.

[It is almost eight years since the above was written. La Vicie passed away, quietly and without effort, December 25, 1959, at the age of 87 years and 8 months.]

# Christine Halverson
## Clay County 1867
## Kimball, Brule Counties 1889
## Lyman County 1889

by her daughter, Helen Halverson

*[Christina Matson Halverson, more familiarly known as Christine, was born in Sweden February 14, 1864. Three years later, in 1867, she left Sweden with her parents and came to the United States, and settled with them on a farm several miles from Vermillion, South Dakota. She lived on the farm during her childhood and girlhood. As a young woman, she spent about a year in Sioux City, Iowa with her brother, Olin, who was a photographer.*

*In the spring of 1889, she came to Kimball to divide her time with her brother Olin who had established the first photography studio in Kimball, and with her brother Matt who was on a ranch in Lyman County. Christina, Olin and Matt all had claims adjoining in Lyman County.]*

It was in these years during which Christina and her brother homesteaded in Lyman County that the struggle between the cattle rustlers and the law-abiding people who were pushing civilization westward reached its culmination. In the western part of the United States were vast cattle ranges, and here is where the rustlers were very plentiful and bold throughout the period of nearly a quarter of a century. At this time, Chamberlain was a small frontier town. Thirty miles south of Chamberlain was Phelps Island, named after Frank Phelps who owned it and made his home there. This island was the rendezvous of one of the worst gangs ever to infest any country. A gang headed by Frank Phelps and his henchman, Henry Schroeder. These rustlers did not want the bottom-land west of river settled for that ruined the outlet for their stolen stock. Boasts had been made that the settlers would soon be driven out.

Directly opposite the island on the west side of the river lived Matt Matson and his sister, Christina. With them lived a twelve year old boy, George McDonald, from an orphan's home in Sioux City. In the fall of 1892, Christina and Matt moved into their new frame house. Their ranch lay in the path used by Phelps and his henchman, Schroeder, and other rustlers.

Christina and her brother watched these operations, and it was not long before Phelps became aware of their observation. On December 28, 1892, Christina Matson filed a complaint against Frank Phelps and Will Spalding for stealing a cow in the fall. The desire to do away with witnesses in this cow-stealing case can easily be called the immediate motivation for the murder of Matt Matson, although the intention was to kill both Christina and Matt.

Immediately Phelps began to harass the Matsons in an effort to drive them away so he would be undisturbed in his cattle stealing. He borrowed sugar, but returned it poisoned. The little boy who was the only one to use sugar in his coffee complained of the taste of the coffee. In this way, Christina discovered that the sugar had been poisoned. The pet dog, King, was poisoned. One day while Christina was herding cattle Schroeder raised his gun several times to shoot her, but was unable to do so. During this winter the threats to the Matsons continued; but threats of any kind, poison or otherwise, made the Matsons more determined to stay. Christina was the immediate target of Phelps and his gang of rustlers because she was very determined to put an end to all of this lawlessness.

Henry Schroeder, the henchman of Phelps and a man who often did odd jobs for Matt Matson, was bribed with $300.00 by Phelps to kill both Christina and her brother.

On May 20, 1893, Christina and her brother received a letter from their brother Olin in Kimball. In the twilight of that evening as Matt rested in the doorway, and Christina sat by the lamp reading the letter and Kimball paper, a shot rang out: Matt fell backward into the house; the firing of the shot extinguished the light from the lamp. Henry Schroeder had earned his $300.00.

At first Christina thought the boy had been hit. Only when the child screamed, did she realize that Matt had been killed.

Through the window she saw the figure of a man and recognized him as Schroeder. About midnight, dressed in her brother's clothes, she tried to get out through a window to go to Felkner's, the nearest neighbor, three miles away; but hearing the click of a trigger she withdrew and spent the rest of the night firing a gun occasionally to keep the man away from the house so he would not set fire to the house or picket fence. The morning after this night of horror, Christina's brown hair was streaked with white and within three weeks was completely white.

At dawn, she sent the little boy to the nearest neighbor. Help presently arrived, and officers came from Chamberlain. Lyman County was unorganized at that time and attached to Brule County of which Chamberlain was the county seat for judicial purposes.

Schroeder made no effort to escape and was arrested. Phelps was arrested as instigator of the crime. The case was tried twice in Lyman County, but Phelps and Schroeder declared the trials were unfair because of the strong feeling in favor of the Matsons in Chamberlain. As a result, a new trial was granted and took place in Alexandria, the county seat of Hanson County.

The Matsons obtained the best legal counsel in the Northwest. Dick Haney, Judge of the Fourth Judicial Circuit, presided over the trial. During the two years the case lasted the court room was packed. Great interest was manifested throughout the Northwest because of the problems which cattle rustling had presented. The case was bitterly contested. Phelps and Schroeder were desperately fighting for their lives, and, on the other hand, the Matsons were determined that all who had been implicated should be punished to the full extent of the law. Judge Haney sentenced Schroeder to life imprisonment and hard labor at the Sioux Falls penitentiary where he died in 1902. Phelps, who was sentenced to hang, died a few weeks after the trial.

The conviction of Phelps, who had been a leader of the rustlers for twenty years, broke up the cattle rustling and left this portion of the frontier open for peaceful development.

# Cora Allen Headding
## Aurora County
## 1876

*[Born in Madison, Wisconsin, Cora Allen moved to Rochester, Minnesota at the age of three, where her father's machinery business did well until a Chinch bug pestilence "consumed or ate every green leaf" in the country and ruined him financially. Homesteading in Dakota Territory on the 360 acres available to him as a Civil War veteran, her father built a sod dugout and brought his family out to the homestead during the summer of 1876.]*

As we traveled along the road from Rochester to South Dakota, we met a farmer who admired our horse team very much; and wanted to know what my father would take for them. Father then asked the farmer what he would give him for them. The farmer answered that he would trade him two yoke of oxen and two cows, which made 6 head of cattle. Father told him it was a trade. (The horses would run away at the twitter of a bird's wing. They were so high strung and nervous, so our nerves were somewhat settled by the trade, because the oxen traveled slowly and contented.)

That evening we arrived at Sioux Falls, a town then consisting of a store and post office combined. This was owned by a man named Vaneps, who later on owned several stores in South Dakota. There was a Blacksmith shop and two or three houses. My father entered the store and soon heard news about the Custer war in the Black Hills [the Battle of the Little Big Horn]; he was very much affected by the news and asked my mother if we should go on. She answered, "we'll go on and meet whatever there is to meet in this wild country, we are pioneers now," and we came the rest of the way to our homestead, which was 75 trackless miles west of Sioux Falls. We finally arrived at the homestead, and the house which father had built the year before. I climbed down from the wagon and looked around at the endless prairie and clapped my hands and exclaimed to father: "Is this all our lots?" For I had been raised in town on a small fenced-in lot for a play ground.

One awful experience was a blacked-out sun for days when clouds of migrating small brown grasshoppers filled the sky between sun and earth. They would descend to earth and would stay until they had devoured everything except the limbs of the timber; they would all rise in a cloud and continue their journey north and supposedly to the Arctic. Coming from South America they came three different summers. Father would have new mown hay in the shock and the piles of hay would be covered so thick that they would be completely colored brown like the grasshoppers.

It happened that the man I was to marry had taken land a mile north of where Mitchell now stands. It is located in a beautiful valley with the Fire Steel Creek running through it. We were married and built our home on his homestead and there my child was born. Misfortune overtook us and my husband passed away in an insane asylum. My child was two years of age. For many years I worked hard to support myself and child for we were left destitute. I educated her and she became a school teacher. When she became twenty one years of age Meade County was opened for settlement, and we both came to the Black Hills in December of 1911, and both took up land side by side. She taught school at Cottonwood that winter, and I procured employment in Rapid City.

My late husband and daughter having passed on before me, I am living alone in Sturgis.

Now my old homestead north of Mitchell is a lake. The City of Mitchell built a large dam across the beautiful Fire Steel Creek, which holds the water that furnishes the water supply for the City. What more could I ask than the memory of my old homestead being put to such wonderful use as furnishing water for thousands of thirsty people?

# Dr. Abbie Ann Hall Jarvis
# Faulk County
# 1880

by her daughter, Annette

*[Abbie Ann Hall was born September 16th, 1854 at Zanesville, Ohio, the second daughter of Dr. and Mrs. Samuel Hall. Later they moved to Reedsburg, Wisconsin, where she was married to Matthew James Jarvis on Christmas day, 1876. They lived in Wisconsin with their two sons where Mr. Jarvis was in the milling business until March 1st, 1880, shortly after which they moved to Redfield, Dakota Territory.]*

The first snow came October 17th. It was a heavy snow and a bad storm raged on for two days and from that time on there wasn't a railroad opened east of Huron only long enough to let a few trains through and then the wind would drift the cuts full again until the company abandoned the effort to keep them clear until Spring. We had all thought all through the summer that we had found the land of no winter; we were assured of this by the Seventy Niners who had spent the past winter down the river. They told us there was no use to hurry about getting up the wood or hauling provisions from Huron as the trips could be made at any time during the winter without discomfort. There was not a day after the 17th of October that it was fit for anyone to try to make the trip of forty miles and after the first of January we were bottled up under four feet of snow and there was no possible chance of getting out until Spring. Before the winter was half over provisions got pretty scarce. But there was this we had to be thankful for: as long as any one of us had anything to eat it was shared with the rest of the little community. There came a time when the sharing played out and there was nothing left to share but wheat ground in a coffee mill and antelope meat. One coffee mill served the five families and they took turns using it. It

60

was owned by Mrs. Welker and was the only one in the neighborhood. The antelope were so very poor, it was almost more than you could take to have to kill them — they would look up at you with their big, sad eyes as they came up to the house for food.

It had been a long time since they had had a match but had been able to keep their fires going by lighting one fire from another. One day, Mrs. Jarvis was looking through some pockets of clothes Mr. Jarvis had not been wearing and she found an old, dirty match. She was so tickled to find it that she immediately turned and lit it to see whether or not it was any good. You can imagine her surprise when she realized what she had done.

We managed the winter without the use of vegetables of any kind and towards the last the sugar, salt, pepper, coffee and tea were unknown.

Mr. Jarvis made snow shoes out of barrel staves and a sleigh from the same barrel. One day he would put on the snow shoes and drag the sleigh three miles and a half to what was then known as Baker's Grove, tie a load of bush on and drag it back the three and a half miles over the snow. Mr. Sadler that day would grind the wheat, shovel the snow so as to get into the sod barn to feed the horses as there was no getting the horses out of the stable. Next day he would make the trip after the wood and Mr. Jarvis do the wheat and snow act.

As all things come to an end, so did the winter of 1880 and 1881. It was not until the first of May that the first train got through to Huron. The snow left everything looking bright and the men were off to Huron for supplies in no time. It was impossible to buy anything to eat in Huron, so they had to wait for the train. When it arrived, Mr. Myers liberally divided the food between the Huron and Redfield people. Mr. Jarvis got a ham, a sack of flour and his share of the groceries and started home. He had been gone for five days and don't you think his wife was anxious to hear the sound of that wagon? The nights were so still that you could hear the wagon for miles before it came in sight. They drove up about eight o'clock. Mrs. Jarvis was out at the line taking in the washing. She dropped everything, hustled that ham and flour in the house and it didn't take her long to prepare one of the very best meals that mortal man ever sat down to — at least that is what they all thought.

With Spring in all its glory, came many people to settle in this new country and Redfield became a thriving little city. Mrs. Jarvis' mother came out that summer to see her, she had heard about the hard time they were having and was one of the very first to get out there. Such a comfort and pleasure it was to have her with them and such cheer she brought into their home. It seemed to Abbie that she could manage the best meal out of absolutely nothing.

One day some men were driving through the country and they stopped to see if they could have dinner with them. Abbie didn't see how it would be possible to feed four hungry men but her mother stepped up and says, "I think I can find something." They were baking bread, that is it was in the pan about ready to be made in loaves. She took the dough and molded it into a sort of a pancake and fried it. You should have seen those men eat those "Choke Dogs" as she called them. They left with many thanks in more ways than one and couldn't understand how fried bread dough could be so good. After they left Abbie says, "Ma, I could not think of a thing we could possibly fix for them. I think you are a wonder."

When she went back that fall she took Matt, the older little boy, with her and kept him there in Wisconsin for the greater part of his third year. When he came back we were living about a mile and a half from Redfield in a little 12 x 16 shanty out on another claim. Mrs. Jarvis was alone there with her two little boys and their life there was as good a deal as you might think. The boys made pets of gophers and cried when a cousin came out and shot one. They had tamed them so that they would come when called. The wind came and nearly blew our shanty away and the prairie fire passed over us and nearly burned us up, thought surely the house was going to be burned. Abbie had a new sewing machine that was her pride and joy, her father had sent it to her early in the summer. So she alone dragged it out on some plowed ground, soaked a piece of old carpet in water and covered the machine with that. The fire seemed to jump around both machine and house and all was saved. It was nothing short of a miracle.

Before they left Redfield their first little girl, Annette, was born in June 1883. She was a premature baby only weighing two and a fourth pounds. She was so tiny a tea cup could have been put over her head or her mother's wedding ring upon her arm. The doctor said they must not expect to raise her, it would be impossible. Baby incubators were unknown at that time. So the little girl was wrapped in cotton, fed with an eye dropper on sugar and water and carried on a pillow for three months with constant care and attention and it is SHE who is writing this little article today after sixty nine years.

Another claim was taken up in Faulk County near the little inland town of DeVoe, and here Mrs. Jarvis spent five more years battling with the elements of farm life in pioneer South Dakota. Mr. Jarvis was on the road most of the time so she was alone a great deal. Time will not allow me to relate the hardships of these days.

Her two little boys had gone to school the morning of the day of the blizzard of 1888, January 12th. It was a night of agony, never to be forgotten, for she did not know where they were and there was no possible way to find out. The storm raged on all through that day and night. The teacher had piled the school children in a sleigh and had started out in the blizzard, such a wild goose chase for they knew not where they were going, but fortunately they were able to follow a fence across the prairie and accidentally hit a hitchingpost which led them to believe they were at the door of a farm house, which was where they were. So they were saved from perishing in the blizzard.

In 1890 they sold the farm at DeVoe and Mr. Jarvis bought a drug store in Faulkton and here they spent the rest of their lives.

Mrs. Jarvis loved the great out-of-doors. She also loved picnics and camping trips. Many times packing her bedding and food, she with her children would go off to the woods. They would pitch their tent, sleep on the ground and listen to the wind in the trees and the call of the birds as they talked with each other through the still of the night. At these times there would be a camp fire where they would boil their coffee, fry their bacon and eggs, and gather around the fire for the story hours. Usually true stories of her own dear childhood and life.

At another time Mrs. Jarvis with her four children left in a covered wagon to visit her sister in southern Nebraska. It was a trip of about three hundred miles and it was difficult to make twenty five miles a day. They would camp by the wayside, usually near a farm house where they might pitch their tent and buy fresh eggs and milk. One day they were driving over a reservation and got lost. They drove on and on trying to find their way out, but had to give up and were obliged to spend the night there. The boys were telling the girls all kinds of wild Indian stories. They got out a little old gun they had inherited and said they would sleep at the door of the tent and drive the Indians away. As they were leaving the next morning they learned that they had been right on the edge of the reservation. At the end of two weeks the Jarvises drove into the little town of Carleton, Nebraska. A forlorn looking lot: tanned, dusty and dirty, and the two boys were sitting on the whippletrees urging the horses on to their destination. It was but a few blocks but it seemed they never would make it. In spite of all this it would have done your heart good to have witnessed the very cordial welcome the five Jarvises received from the nine cousins and sister. They were greeted with "Here they come! Here they come! Oh! Oh! Aunt Abbie, Aunt Abbie!" We were, of course, late in getting thru and they had been looking for days for the covered wagon. Many happy days followed, with a camping trip down on the river. This time there were sixteen in the group. After the horses (which they thought would never be able to make the trip back) had rested and gained a little from the huge green pastures of Nebraska, the Jarvises left via caravan for South Dakota after a wonderful time and a glorious vacation – if you could call it that – and in due time were home again.

Now since you know something of the hardy pioneer life that Mrs. Jarvis spent with her husband in this country, I want to deal more particularly with the noble services and sacrifices of his good wife, Dr. Abbie A. Jarvis. Her real heroism did not cease with the passing of early pioneer days. As the territory surrounding Faulkton became thickly populated, Mrs. Jarvis beheld more and more the sickness and suffering of her fellow creatures, many of whom were left without proper medical care, owing to the scarcity of trained physicians in this locality. The need pressed more and more heavily on her heart until finally she decided to do that which was uppermost in her mind and something she had always wanted to do above all else at what ever cost. You will note that she had been out of school for at least seventeen years and raised a family. During these past months she had spent what time she could spare studying with her father, who was a doctor. He would often talk his cases over with her. With what knowledge she gathered in this way, she took her two little girls and made her way to Chicago and entered the Woman's Medical College, where she was accepted to begin a four year course of medical training. That was all that was required at that time.

You can well imagine the discouragements of those trying years in school. Here she, with no college education, was entering along with young girls just out of school, vivacious and full of life, they seemed to have everything it takes. But again and again her spirit of the heroic pioneer days asserted itself and she labored on. Her father was practicing in Faulkton, South Dakota during this time making it possible for her to practice during her vacations under his supervision. In this way she was able to earn enough each summer to carry her on thru the following college year. Consequently she earned her way through school. She was obliged to stay home two full years on account of the sickness and death of her mother. But she returned to her studies the following year, taking her little girls with her, she rented a room and did light housekeeping. At the end of that school year in June, 1898, she graduated fourth in her class out of a group of twenty-four.

Returning from the University she began her practice in the city of Faulkton, her own home town. The practice of medicine during those years not only required the knowledge of medicine, but demanded a working understanding of the surrounding country (with the stars as a guide) along with an appreciation of good horse flesh. The contact between patient and doctor was often times a distance of many miles over a dirt road, driven with team and buggy.

It did not take long for those who watched her progress to know that she was a remarkable physician and that the same urge which carried her thru a difficult medical course was present to make her practice a success, which she continued thru the rest of her life. She was, for many years, the first licensed Woman Physician in South Dakota and also the first licensed Woman Pharmacist in South Dakota. Her practice grew from day to day until far and wide she became known for her success in her field. Neither the hot days of the summer nor the stinging frosts and blizzards of the winter kept her from going where duty called her. No trip was too long, no sufferer too poor to keep Dr. Jarvis from those who needed her. Service rather than reward, ever prompted her in her profession. The poorest patient received the best medical care that the doctor could give.

Among her first patients was a ten year old boy who had typhoid fever. The family lived about eight miles out in the country and he had been sick for some time before she was called. On her second visit she found that he was no better so decided to take her father out with her next day. He said that she had properly diagnosed the case and was giving and doing everything that could be done, but that he was a very sick boy and he did not think that he would get well. It was with a prayer and a heavy heart that she left that home that day. The following morning she returned to find no improvement. She was afraid, and as she sat down on the edge of his bed to administer to him, she shook so that her knees were knocking against each other to make a sound much resembling that of a dog flopping his tail upon the floor. And all at once the boy's mother says "My goodness! That dog has got in the house again, he must be under the bed," so down she went to find him. But there was no dog and Dr. Jarvis quietly changed her position and managed to keep herself under better control. No one was the wiser, for she never told. Within a few days the boy passed on.

Although Dr. Jarvis was supposed to have a driver, many, many times she went alone, usually because she preferred to, rather than to have some one waiting around for her. There wasn't any place for a strange man in a small pioneer home when the stork was about to arrive. So she would venture out alone. She was caught in many bad storms, the cold blizzards in the winter and the dust, winds, heat and rain in the summer.

One night she was caught in a regular cloudburst and had to drive up along side of a haystack to wait until morning and day light before she could go on. When she finally got there she was soaked through and through. They loaned her clothes while her own were drying. Soon the stork arrived with a bouncing boy and everybody was happy.

Another time when she was driving alone her horses ran into a barb wire fence that had been stretched across the road, and the tongue of the buggy hit the post in such a way as to throw her out head first on the ground between the wheels of the buggy. Her first thought was "Well, I guess that I'm killed this time." Then she tried to move a little. First she pushed back her head, then her arm, and then stretched out a leg and found that she could move alright, so decided she wasn't hurt after all, got up, led her horses on over a mile or so to one small light that glowed into what was otherwise pitch darkness. When she arrived at the little hut from which the light had shone she found a man living there alone. He was rather hesitant about asking her in, so she finally said, "Well I guess that I will have to stay all night. I can't go on." He replied that he was there alone, but Dr. Jarvis answered." I am not afraid of you if you are not afraid of me." So she stayed.

It was a familiar sight to see Dr. Jarvis on the street with her white apron and little black satchel. Everybody knew and loved her and would stop for a little chat with her. Especially the little children were ready with a happy "Hello, Aunt Abbie" and then sidling up to her would invariably ask, "Do you have a little baby in that satchel?" You see, the mothers would tell the children that Dr. Jarvis brought the babies in her little satchel. So you can understand why that was a very important satchel. One time there was a family who had lost their little baby that she had left for them, it was a very tiny little baby and their little girl slipped up to her and said, "Aunt Abbie, we want you to leave us another little baby." She tho't that she would, and the dancing eyes looked up at Aunt Abbie and said "But next time please leave us a larger one."

Dr. Jarvis was not very observing, that is her mind was so intent on her profession that she would do little things without thinking. One day two little girls were sitting in front of a store, and they saw her coming. First one would giggle and then the other, then they would look up at her and both would giggle again, so as she came nearer to them she said, "Well now girls it couldn't be you are laughing at me?" She could hardly keep her own face straight. They said that they were and started to giggle again. So she said, "Well, what is wrong?" They told her she had her hat on backwards and sure enough she had. It was one of those hats that made a lot of difference which way it was worn.

Years passed on and during this time her oldest boy was accidentally killed and within two years she lost the younger daughter. These were sorrows from which she never fully recovered. Others she had helped and saved yet for her own loved ones she was helpless and could do nothing. Such a feeling of helplessness and despair. But for her "the show must go on." Through pathos, sorrow and joys she went ever onward, diligently performing those services which were so dear to her. Scarcely a family in the whole country side had not been helped by her services, her understanding and her helpful ways.

During these years it had been a great cross to Dr. Jarvis to think that she had never been Grandmother. She dearly loved children and she didn't see why she wasn't a Grandmother. Mrs. Brydon was Grandmother, Mrs. Warner was Grandmother, Mrs. Bottum was Grandmother and why in the world, couldn't SHE be Grandmother too?

One dark cloudy night in April the phone rang and she was called to help the stork on its way to a family where she had often been before. Before she could get her clothes on the phone rang again. This time it was a call way on beyond the place where the first call came from and they too were looking for the stork. She explained to these people that she would have to go to the first call first and if it was possible to leave there for awhile she would hurry on to them and take care of the first call on her way back.

These were automobile days. Quite an improvement over Horse and Buggy days. When she reached this first home she found that she could do just as she had suggested and that there would be plenty of time. Annette was her Chauffeur, but they tho't they had better send a driver along in case of trouble etc., so that is what they did. So off we went out into one of the blackest nights and nobody seemed to know anything about where we were going. We went on and on, seemed like we would never come to any place that was at all familiar and all of a sudden we found we were right upon a great Lake and no road leading anywhere, and lo and behold—just as we were at our wits end, a voice called from across the lake, "Dr. Jarvis is that you?" She immediately answered that it was, and again came the voice, "Stay right where you are and I will come and get you." So we were led away from the lake, over to the home upon the hill. There was nothing but dim lights to show the way. She climbed upon the steps, on in the kitchen and then up some steep steps into a little room, and there She was GRANDMOTHER!

How gloriously happy she was. Now she was Grandmother too. Nice big eight pound baby girl. A war baby, her Daddy was in France, and he was to name the baby. But time was precious and she must hurry on so after she had taken care of the mother and the baby was washed and cared for, she had to be on her way again to the other mother and this time she beat the stork by several hours, but when he did arrive he left a nice big boy.

When the name came from across the seas for this little girl, she was to be called Annette, which especially pleased her Aunt. Annette was nine months old when her Daddy got back from France and that day she took her first step, so we said she walked out to meet him.

In spite of her cheerful and seemingly untiring nature age was creeping upon her and as the years rolled by she became less active. She reluctantly gave up her downtown office and set up an office in her home. It was with a great deal of sorrow that she left the office in which she had been so long. She continued to practice, it was surprising the number of people who clung to her for help and relief. The faith which they had established in her never waned. It was to her they would inevitably go. Her years of service were fulfilled. She had, although she didn't fully realize it, attained her highest ideal. She had performed innumerable services to mankind. She fell victim to that most vicious disease, cancer, and endured great suffering with that patience and courage she had ever displayed in her life. On a quiet day in early May 1931, she passed away; but with her passing went the finest of pioneers. The influence she had upon the community was of extremely wide scope. Nowhere is such service more clearly exemplified than in her life.

It is such sturdy pioneers as she that led to the great development and modernization of the west. Those pioneers were the ones that taught and vividly portrayed service to humanity in the greatest degree.

## BIRDS
### Dr. Abbie Jarvis

*(This is a true story written by Dr. Jarvis as she jogged home one early morning after a night in the country by the bedside of a very sick patient. Lady Bug was the horse she drove.)*

After a night spent in an overheated room by the bed-side of the sick, your nerves all on edge from worry and work and about as depressed as you can very well be. What a joy it is to step out in the Great Out of Doors and get in your buggy, gather the lines and say to little "Lady Bug," "Come, old girl, we are going home at last." Taking in a long breath of the pure air, that acts like magic on your over-wrought nerves and be greeted by a beautiful song. "Oh! I am so happy this morning, I am so happy." An answer comes, "So am I, So am I." Looking around to see from whence comes this cheer, I see Mr. Meadow Lark, with his gray coat, yellow vest and black necktie, cocking his head first on one side and then the other looking through his black eyes at you, as if saying, "I am so happy, why are not you?" You answer him and say, "You dear little fellow, I am happy for am I now going HOME."

As if in keeping with all the rest, the world seems aglow with light and beauty, the sun peeping above the horizon sending millions and millions of golden shafts over the prairie, changing the dew drops that are hanging on the blades of grass, and the fine silken webs of the spiders into a whole world of diamonds and everything in nature smiles. You raise your eyes in adoration and say, "Surely God is good and wonderful, how glad I am to be alive and with the larks. I am so happy." The depression of the night's watching and waiting are for a time forgotten and you just relax and give way to the influence of the bright morning.

A little further on and another sweet song greets your ear as the sky lark flies above with a burst of song, trailing back like the tail of a meteor as it sails through the air, spreading good cheer and joy. It really is contagious and you laugh for very joy and say, "Oh! you dear, sweet thing, do keep right on singing and take your happiness to all sorrow laden hearts."

Off in the distance you hear the boom, boom of the prairie chicken as he struts off to greet the morning and see what he can find for breakfast. I suppose the little wife is at home fixing the fire to take care to cook whatever he brings home and taking care of her little brood or sitting on her nest keeping the eggs warm waiting patiently for the little chicks to come forth.

And now we hear the churip, churip of the little sparrow as they work building their home and making a place to raise their little ones.

Passing a little grove we hear the chatter of the Blackbirds. They are surely a sociable lot, as they fly around in great flocks and light on some newly plowed ground catching bugs and worms to make a breakfast for the mother bird and their little ones. He is really a pretty little fellow with his shiny black coat and bright red wings. Even the "Caw, Caw" of the old black crow is music to our ear THIS NICE MORNING WHEN WE ARE SO GLAD WE ARE GOING HOME TO OUR NEST, and we can imagine that we can hear him say unto his mate, "I know where there is something good for you to eat."

YOU, Mr. Robin! red breast, where did you come from? Any one would think that we loved you best of all, and I believe we do. Where did you get this nice grey suit with that red vest and that sweet song of "Cheer up, Cheer up" of yours? When we hear it we know Spring is not far away and that you have come to enliven our rainy day. You do not seem the least bit timid, just hop across the lawn, nearly up to our very door. After he has established a home among us he will return again year after year and build his home in our trees. As Craig Thomas says; "Drink and bathe from our pan to let us know he is renewing the contract that we made with him last year, that we would provide the water if he would provide the rollicking Good Cheer."

As we drive along we pass by a little grove of trees, out of which pounces Mr. King bird swooping down trying to peck poor little Lady Bug on the head, as if he was angry for being disturbed, and tries to drive her away.

On the opposite side of the road we see the cattle browsing the tender grass as if they were trying with the others to get their breakfast. Everything seems quiet and tranquil while the Buffalo birds are perched on their backs or following along in their wake after their breakfast. I do not know as they sing or make much of any noise, they are often seen among the cattle, the male bird is black with head and neck dark brown, the female is smaller and duller in color. It does not build any nests but lays its eggs in other birds nests and leaves the eggs to be hatched by their foster mothers.

I have noticed many pretty yellow birds, I suppose wild canaries, and a very pretty blue bird with bright red breast who have come and seem quite at home with us.

And now we note with regret that the Autos have come to supersede Little Lady Bug and the buggy. We whiz along so fast we can not see or hear our little friend, just glide along, hurry – hurry – hurry, to get to our patients and then home again. I sometimes long to gather up the lines again and jog along listening to the different sounds and music of the farmers as they work in the fields and to hear the birds singing.

As the sun sinks in the west, spreading its golden light over the sky, we listen to the sleepy songs of the little fellow as it grows fainter and fainter as one by one they put their heads under their wings and all is quiet, and in the great silence we bow head and give thanks to the One from whom all good gifts come and for our mercies and our pleasures.

## Myrta Crystal Miller Jones
## Bon Homme County
## 1878

Since Mother was 14 years old when she came to South
Dakota, most of her experiences as a pioneer came after
her marriage to Silas S. Jones, at the little town of Bon
Homme on December 25, 1879, when she was 15 years old.

Her husband was a stockman and did some farming.
He also supplemented his income by hauling freight with
oxen from Yankton to the Indian Agency at Greenwood.
He learned to speak the Sioux language and was a friend
of the Indians. During the early years of their marriage they
lived in the vicinity of Tyndall. Many hardships were encountered during the cold winters in Bon Homme County
as they lived part of the time in a sod and a log house.
Especially difficult was the winter of 1888 when South Dakota
had the worst blizzard in history. No trains came to Tyndall
from early fall until May 1889. Many Christmas gifts from
distant relatives were received in July.

Supplies dwindled during the long winter, and neighbors
shared their surplus with those less fortunate. There was
no kerosene and their only light through the long winter
evenings came from the open door of the stove. Candles
were scarce and used sparingly.

Seven children were born to my parents — four sons and
three daughters — so Mother always was busy taking care
of her family. My father was a good provider but sometimes
it was difficult with so many to feed and clothe.

One year I especially remember when we were in
"straightened circumstances," Mother, Sister Belle and I pulled
and topped turnips for a neighbor, receiving half the turnips
for our work. Those we used all winter as a substitute for
potatoes. Our only meat was mutton, and we had no butter
and very little milk. Regardless we seemingly thrived though
Mother liked neither turnips nor mutton afterwards.

About 1896 Father felt the urge to go farther west, so the family started out with 4 covered wagons, quite a few extra horses and about 35 head of cattle; Mother and Father drove the wagon teams, the boys drove the cattle, and Sister Belle and I, although very young, rode horse back and kept the loose horses with the wagon train.

We usually camped early, giving the boys time to get the cattle to camp before dark. Father would pitch the tent and Mother would busy herself preparing supper for the family. She cooked on a small stove with an oven in the pipe and we always had hot biscuits for supper. We had a folding table and chairs but usually ate and cooked out-of-doors unless it was raining.

Our beds were made on the ground inside the tent, where we slept soundly and well, except in case of storm, when Mother and Father held the tent poles to keep it from falling down.

We drove to Oacoma, Rapid City and on to Viewfield, Meade County, in the extreme western part of the state. Grazing land always was available and we camped near streams or rivers as we needed water for the stock and our own use. Sometimes we would spend several days or even weeks in one place. Often we traveled with other families and Mother enjoyed the companionship of the women, exchanging ideas and recipes with them as we do today, although I imagine they were somewhat different.

Mother was a true pioneer, working early and late, helping with the stock when necessary, even taking turns watching them at night. One evening when she was watching the herd, after an especially difficult day, she fell asleep on the grass. She wasn't asleep long, however, before she was rudely awakened by several of the cattle smelling of her face and person. It was a tense moment because no matter how frightened she was of what might happen to her lying there under their hoofs she knew she must move carefully and slowly thus eliminating the danger of stampeding the whole herd. After what seemed hours of nosing and investigating her position and being, the cattle, satisfied that she was not harmful, departed to their original position with the rest of the herd.

One night some ranchers came to our camp for help to fight one of the worst enemies of the pioneer, the prairie fire. When one was in the general vicinity all people turned out to fight the monster lest it grow in fierceness and velocity and burn them all out. Also one never refused to help one's fellowman when he needed assistance from the elements. My mother and whole family, with the exception of my sister and I, left to fight the blaze. We remained at camp with an older girl to await their return. When the morning light came, our mother, with the rest of the family, came home to camp: tired, dirty and bedraggled, but happy they had been able to squelch the fire and help others.

When Father sold his cattle he did not put his money in banks, but brought it all home. Most of it was in gold so Mother made a canvas belt just wide enough for a $20 gold piece. This she filled and wore around her waist day and night. One night when Father had gone for supplies and she was alone with the children; she was awakened suddenly when she felt the weight of the belt slip from her body. Frightened she lay quietly for some time, then investigated and found the belt had simply come unfastened. There was great relief in recovering the money but little rest for her the remainder of the night thinking of what might have happened.

At one time Father had a large flock of sheep, and whenever we camped at night they lay as near to the tent as possible. One night they had crowded in so closely they were nearly pushing the tent down, and when Mother tried pushing them away they became frightened and stampeded into the darkness. Mother and Father dressed and taking lighted lanterns started after them. Sheep like a light, and the sound of my mother's voice calling to them in the night calmed their fears sufficiently to enable my parents to drive them back to camp.

Our camp usually was pitched near creeks or rivers where plenty of dry wood was available for our camp fire. One chilly night in early November Mother and the boys carried a large quantity of wood up to the camp. One large hollow log they singled out as they thought it would hold fire during the night. About supper time Father put the log on the fire and in a short time out came a huge hissing rattlesnake, writhing in the hot coals. Father took a long pole and kept it from crawling out of the fire where it soon burned to a crisp. Having watched the episode we children were so frightened and excited we had little appetite left for our supper.

Out on the range there were few schools and because of the distance, hazardous weather conditions and the fact attendance was not compulsory, we sometimes had only a three months term in summer. Then during the winter Father would rent a house in town for six months so we could attend more regularly. My older sister, Emma, always made her home in Tyndall with her grandparents thus making it possible to secure her education there.

We came back to Tyndall in 1898 and remained there about two years then started back again to Oacoma in early fall. We had a large flock of sheep so had to travel slowly. My brothers had remained in Oacoma so Sister and I drove the sheep and Mother and Father the covered wagons.

The first day we traveled about 25 miles and camped that night at the home of a friend about seven miles southeast of Wagner. This man had a small farm of 60 acres near his own for sale and talked Father into buying it. Mother's only comment, "If we buy this farm, I'll never move again." So they bought it, but did move again when they went to Wagner in January 1907.

A few days before her death, I went to the hospital to see her and after my greeting she hastened to say, "I've something to tell you," and as she spoke her face was beautiful with inner rapture yet with a longing that I might understand and believe what she had to say.

"An angel came to see me last night! It was dressed in thin, white, misty material and stood just inside my door. I said, 'Are you looking for some one?' and the angel looked at me and smiled sweetly but said nothing. 'Surely you did not come to see me?' I asked, and then it came closer and smiled again, then disappeared."

It was a wonderful experience, and justified her faith, as she was given a glimpse of the heaven she was soon to share. Three days later on September 25, 1948, she died at the age of 83 years, 11 months and 8 days, and was buried in the Wagner cemetery.

Her unfailing courage, love and devotion to family, friends and all people endears her in the hearts of many. Her heart was as big as the wind swept prairie on which she pioneered and her faith in her God as firm and true as the earth on which she traveled with covered wagon. She knew the trials and hardships of the pioneer and the great joy and peace that comes from unselfish living. That is the wonderful heritage that she has left to those of us who knew and loved her.

# Mary Agnes Kessler
## Lake County
## 1861

*[Mary Agnes Kessler was born in Dubuque County, Iowa on May 15, 1861. Her father had left Germany at the age of seventeen because he objected to the military training required of young men. Mary was married to Dennis William Sullivan and the bride and groom came by train to Dakota Territory, locating seven miles northeast of Madison where they had purchased the Olmore homestead.]*

In August 1886, a six months old boy had died of brain fever which had resulted from a siege of whooping cough. The family now consisted of two dear little boys who were two and three years old.

The spring of 1887 was cold and rainy and the Sullivans were late with the spring planting. On May 14, they began to plant corn. Mary had done the house work and cared for the children and decided to help in the field since there was need of haste.

When she left the house, she admonished Jacob and Francis to stay inside. After one row had been planted, Mary looked toward the house and saw that all was well. When she looked a short time later, the house was in flames.

The fire had started in the opposite side of the house and the neighbors on that side were there before Mary and Dennis could get home.

After having tried in vain to enter the burning house and rescue her boys, the frantic mother turned and ran, never stopping until she had reached Madison seven miles away where her favorite sister-in-law lived. She and Dennis stayed there until after the double funeral of the little boys who had burned in the fire. They were placed in one casket and all that told the identity of them was an arm showing the sleeve of the garment worn that day.

Kind neighbors moved a two room house to the foundation where the other house had been and helped Mary and Dennis get started again and here, six weeks later, Joseph was born.

# "Aunt Sadie"
## Sarah Ann Klebsch
## Spink County
## 1879

Sarah Ann Klebsch was born in Museoda, Wisconsin in 1866, the third daughter in a family of eleven children. She arrived in Huron, South Dakota with her Mother, two brothers and two sisters in the summer of 1879 at the age of thirteen years. At that time Huron consisted of a depot, a grocery store combined with a meat market and a post office. They were fortunate to find one small room in the crowded hotel, where the six of them spent their first night in South Dakota. After their breakfast of baked beans, corn bread and black coffee they climbed into a lumber wagon and started their journey. The seats in the wagon were only trunks and boxes and it was pulled by two slow old horses. This was the way they made their way to Redfield, which was to be their home.

The sun was hot and the dust blew as the young girl, who was to live so long in this new territory, rode slowly along. They forded the James River and arrived at last to the dugout which had a dirt roof and a board floor. Like so many pioneer people the Ware family settled on the bank of the James River. She has described it as very beautiful with the trees and miles and miles of level prairie covered with wild grass waving in the winds. The river provided them with an abundance of water and the fishing and hunting supplemented their meager diet. They also found wild grapes, plums and buffalo berries, which were used to good advantage. Their nearest source of food supply was Huron.

Aunt Sadie had the misfortune to lose her mother in 1881. She went to Vinton, Iowa, finished her education and then returned to South Dakota where she married a young farmer, Ernest Klebsch, in 1884.

She was a natural born leader in her community. With seven children of her own she felt the need of religious and social activities. She promoted the first Sunday School, which was held at the Little Red School House, and helped organize "The Busy Bee" one of the oldest rural ladies club in Spink County. Neighbors and friends began fondly calling her "Aunt Sadie," and the name became hers for all of her life.

From early childhood she was interested in caring for the sick and became a skillful nurse. As the years went by the whole community depended on her help. She especially liked taking care of mothers-to-be, and helped bring more than 100 babies into this world. One time, during a bad blizzard, she delivered a baby alone by directions from the Doctor given by telephone. During the flu epidemic of 1918, Aunt Sadie did a great amount of nursing all around the neighborhood. Whenever an accident happened or someone was taken quite ill, she was the first one they called to come and help out. She was able to live alone and do most of her own work until she was almost 90 years old.

As she grew older she enjoyed writing about her early experiences here in South Dakota. Following are some incidents written in her own words:


One time at about the age of 15 years as I was walking through the woods along the James River, my attention was attracted to some wild grapes overhanging the water on the opposite side of the river. There were several large rocks in the river and I determined to cross the water on these rocks in an effort to get the grapes. The water was deep and the current very swift and in watching the water I became dizzy and fell into the river. I sunk to the bottom and remember just how it looked down there. In a short time I came to the surface and someone soon grabbed my collar and I was pushed forward by this person who was swimming behind me.

When we reached the shore I was pulled out, stood on my feet and shaken severely. This person then disappeared in the thicket. He was a very tall, erect, young Indian man who had rescued me. I was not aware of his presence at the time I fell into the water and I never knew the purpose of the shaking. I always felt, however, that the Indians were my friends and found them a very interesting people.

Another time while walking through the woods I chanced upon an Indian skull lying on the ground. In the branches of a nearby tree were the other bleached bones of the Indian skeleton. It was the custom of this people to wrap their dead in blankets and place them in trees. Flood waters the following spring washed the skeleton from this tree and all traces were gone.

The first year on our claim my family raised enough potatoes and rutabagas for our own use. We also had a cow which supplied sufficient milk for our needs. The following winter was exceedingly cold and snow very deep, which prevented us from getting our supplies. Consequently, we had no meat, sugar, coffee, flour and other staple foods, but lived approximately three months on muffins and pancakes made from wheat which we ground on a hand coffee mill. This grinding was a very slow process and kept one person busy most of the time. We also had potatoes, rutabagas, and milk and fortunately had plenty of fire wood.

One morning, not long after we came to Dakota, I looked out across the prairie and saw what I thought to be a huge herd of sheep. I watched it for several days and decided to investigate. I started on foot in that direction. The distance proved to be much farther than I had anticipated when I started, as one could see many miles across the prairie. I came closer and I found that my "herd of sheep" consisted of bleached skulls and bones of buffalo. At least 100 of these animals had been slaughtered by white hunters for their hides only; the meat having been a total waste.

Actions such as this could not be tolerated by the Indians. They were justified in defending themselves from people who showed so little consideration for them and their property which they have cherished for so long.

Indians were a very conservative people. They never killed for sport. If they were in need of meat they would kill only enough to satisfy their needs. They considered the buffalo, antelope and other game theirs, much the same as the farmer of to-day considers his herds and flocks. Their rivers and streams were well stocked with fish and yet the Indian and his family were always amply supplied with what they needed.

My parent's claim was located on the James River, nearby an Indian camping ground. An Indian trail, which ran through this farm, could be seen for miles across the prairie. We lived in a sod shanty and our closest railroad station, from which we procured all our provisions, was a distance of 45 miles. A round trip to this point during inclement weather required more than two days and, of course, we traveled with horses and wagons.

The reproduction of the Council Stone, which still stands on the extreme southern portion of my farm was, to the Indians, the object of much meditation and reflection. On one occasion it was my privilege to witness an interesting ceremonial around this stone. As I remember, the chief led the eight men through a narrow passageway and all gathered in circular formation about this stone. They then sat on the ground and folded their arms. The chief was the first to smoke his pipe. He then passed it to the one on his right and each one in turn smoked it until it reached the fourth Indian, who returned it to the chief. The chief then passed it to the one on his left, and after the last one had finished smoking it was returned to the chief. The chief then wrote something on the stone and they all departed. Not a word had been spoken or a sound uttered during the entire ceremony, which I judge lasted about thirty minutes. When they were out of sight, I went to see what had been written, but of course I could not decipher the strange marks.

In the year of 1892 the original council stone was stolen from the Klebsch farm. Since that time I have tried to establish something to preserve the memory of the council stone and vicinity in which it was located by the Indians. This past year in 1939 with the help of Mr. Lester Black, of Redfield we have made a reproduction of the stone. The members of the D. A. R. furnished the material and the place was fenced in.

This monument that was made to the honor of the Old Council Stone now stands in the school yard of the N.W. ¼ of Section 25-17-64, only about 20 rods south of its original location.

# Anna Charlotta Bror Lindberg
## Brown County
## 1883

On telling the life story of Anna Charlotta Bror Lindberg one has to start at the very beginning of her life, to get an accurate background for the story.

Being born Dec 12, 1839 at Hjortquam, Sweden of poor tenant farmers with a large family, where the women folks, as well as the men, had to work out doors to make a living. the soil was very poor, and of course no machinery except a walking plow, a wagon and some oxen to work with. It was necessary for her, at the age of nine to do the simple cooking for the family over an open fireplace where the heat from the fire was right in her face; as far as schooling was concerned it was limited to a few short terms, to learn the three R's, and as she got a little older there was nothing to do; where there were large families the older ones had to get out to work in families either on the farm or in town. She told that a girl at that time got fifty kroner a year and keep, which would be about $12.00 of our money. While thus engaged she had the misfortune to injure her hand with a fish bone and blood-poisoning set in and the doctor despaired of her getting over it, unless the hand was taken off; but in despair she went to a quack doctor who with his ointments healed her hand but it left her right hand crippled with bent fingers and not very strong and as the saying is "misfortune never comes single" her fiance broke off their engagement, on this account.

Now, not having anything to keep her in the old Country, and as there was quite an emigration to America she decided to come here. Borrowing enough money to get a ticket, she started with a few companions for Chicago; at that time they were still using the slow going, wooden steamboats, which took more than two weeks to cross the ocean; and when the storm blew hard at night the boat would creak in every joint and when the boat went down the high waves it seemed like it never would stop until it got to the bottom of the ocean. Finally, reaching Chicago after a long tedious journey, she with the others were unloaded at the depot; the rest had friends and relatives, but she having none was left by her companions. I couldn't call them friends, sitting alone in a strange place unable to talk to anyone; but after awhile a stranger, who could talk her language, came and took her home and kept her until she was able to get a place to work and pay back her friends who advanced her money for her ticket.

This was in the spring of 1871; her employer was a grocery store man; when the "big Chicago Fire" broke out, he went to see what the outlook was; when he came back he said "nothing will save Chicago now"! So he loaded up his delivery wagon full of goods and took her along, taking them across the river to a park, for her to watch the goods until the fire was over. I will digress to tell something about the fire. It was no doubt started in a barn by a cow kicking a lamp over; they sold photos showing it afterwards. The firemen put the barn fire out but it was a very dry fall and everything dry as tinder, and no doubt some fire had been left in manure, as when a hard wind came from the South it blew firebrands from there in the night it seemed, and before the Fire Department could get there the fire was beyond control. After the fire the man she was employed by started a tavern and it was here she met her future husband, he was employed in the Steel Mills. They, of course, had to rent a place to live in on the start. In the meantime three children were born.

The winter of 1883 the Steel mills were shut down, and some of their friends were telling about the farm land in Dakota, that you could get free just by living on it five years, the best land in the world. So her husband, with a nephew, left for Dakota Territory to take up a Homestead; of course they were just going to stay the five years, then return to Chicago. They landed in Groton but were told that a Rail Road was to be built North from Andover, so they went twelve miles North of Andover and each squatted on a claim as the land was not surveyed yet. Having built a small house, her husband sent for her and the children to come out, arriving the 10th of April 1883. I don't know whether all the vissitudes and disappointments have a place in this record or not; but the summer of 1883 was very dry, no rain coming until August 3rd, when a hard rain and hailstorm hit. When the Fall came the Township was surveyed, it was found that some of the squatters had two houses on a quarter section and others had none. They had to move their house, also their Nephew's. As the potatoes and rutabagas had not come up until after the August 3rd. rain, they made a fast growth so made a fair crop and the corn planted on sod made a fair growth and made some fodder. Hay was put up from the sloughs so the stock was well provided for, which was well as the winter set in about Thanksgiving, a long hard winter with lots of snow. A few cold days and then a three days blizzard, and under those conditions her husband was taken mentally ill and had to be taken to a hospital, where he passed away in about three years, leaving her all alone with her three children.

There was not so much broken on her claim and her nephews quarter. Her nephew, who had lived with her, put her crop in and the crop was good that year. But as usual misfortune never comes singly. When she was out helping her nephew clean out the well, the house caught fire and before any one could do anything it burned down. Not a stitch of clothing was saved and what money she had to live on went with the rest. Now she was left out on the open prairie with nothing but the canopy of Heaven over her head, with three young boys clinging to her skirts. But things never get so bad but they could have been worse. Kind people in Andover contributed money to make a payment on material towards a house, also used clothing was contributed, food was sent out; kind neighbors hauled material out and helped build another house.

After those misfortunes she got discouraged and decided to go back to Chicago. When she arrived there she found her sister in bed with inflammatory rheumatism so she stayed with her and nursed her and took care of her children until spring, then she started a Boarding House, which she ran for a year. But she saw there was no future in that and she thought there would be a better opportunity for her boys in Dakota, so she came back and filed on the claim her husband had filed on. Taking in washing, doing housecleaning and helping her neighbors, she managed to keep things going; in the meantime she had bought a cow and she bought calves and when they were grown she bought a wagon and plow and seeder and her oldest boy, who had been working out, came home to farm. This was in 1889, the first crop failure the Dakotas ever had. She sowed 60 bushels of wheat and harvested 100 bushels, not a very encouraging start, but the younger boys had gotten where they could work out and earn something and she was still taking in washing so there was no hardship, but a lot of hard work.

The oldest boy in the fall of 1891 got discouraged, not getting any crop to speak of, and went back to Chicago. The next oldest boy, Axel, getting tired of working out, wanted to come home and farm; so he put in the crop in 1892, and was the turning point for better times. But things were not all roses. Charley got work in a packing plant in Chicago which he could not stand and not feeling good he returned home to Dakota helping in harvest, doing some threshing; but his health kept getting worse proving to be Quick Consumption and when the snow went off in the spring and the water was running in the draws he passed away. Like the hardy pioneers she suppressed her grief and she and her next oldest boy kept on farming. By hard work and sacrifice, they farmed together until they had one of the largest farms with good improvements and fine equipment and a fine line of live stock.

The youngest boy, in the mean time, decided he would go to Chicago and be employed there, which he did, staying twelve years, getting married while there, his mother turned over her house in Chicago to him. But success having come to his mother and brother, and he was getting nowhere, he wanted to come back and farm so his mother sold her improved quarter section to Axel and turned this money over to him, who used it and the money he got for the house in Chicago to buy a well improved farm here. Mrs. Lindberg, feeling she had no more claim on Axel, moved over with him. She helped her son John what she could and except for a couple of illnesses she was spry and in good shape until she was 92 years old, when she fell and broke her hip. At first it looked like she would get well but gangrene set in and so ended a long and useful life.

# Caroline Junker Lund
## Yankton County
## 1870

*[Caroline Junker was born in Denmark in 1852. She and her husband homesteaded in the district between Volin and Wakonda. Mr. Lund built a house of logs gathered from along the Missouri river and hauled to his homestead site by ox team. They also worked their land by ox team and hauled their winter supply of wood from the Missouri river. In 1877, Mr. Lund bought the land three miles south of Gayville, on the Yankton county side of the county line. This made their home closer to Mrs. Lund's parents. Here they weathered the flood of 1881. They told of living upstairs and watching the water creep up the stairway. They burned their supply of corn that they had stored for seed, and without an oven to bake bread, Mrs. Lund fried the dough. They had just put in a supply of meat so they did not suffer from lack of food. Six children were born to Mr. and Mrs. Lund.]*

This is a copy of the diary of Caroline Junker. The family did not know she had this diary until years later. It was yellow with age and written in the Danish language. Her daughter, Mrs. Sena (Lund) Miller and her niece, Mrs. Hannah (Junker) Sorensen, translated it to the best of their ability.

### Caroline Junker's Diary

March 6, 1869

My dear brother Ole left his home land of Denmark and sailed away to that new and rich land of America. God be with you. Name of the ship he sailed on was Sagominde.

C. Junker.

Kolsnop, June 2, 1870 Ach (1 year, 3 months later)

I leave my childhood home and follow him, my brother, to that new land. God in heaven help me that I may never regret this move, may lead us and help us on our way. For eighteen years I have had all my joys and sorrows here. Never shall I forget the time I've spent here. Farewell, farewell all you dear trees that I have planted. Farewell, farewell my dear home. Adieu, Adieu, Adieu.

C. Junker.

Lekskov, June 3, 1870, 2:30 P.M.

Now we are on our way, have left our home, the parting was sad. It is over with and now I must write a letter to my brother in America and so is my cousin going to write. This is all for today.

C. Junker.

Lekskov, Pentecost Sunday, June 5, 1870.

This morning I attended church services in Nustrop church, most likely for the last time. Provost Bladel used the text from Acts 22, 10th chapter, verses 42 and 48 and John 3, 16, "For God so loved the world that he gave His only begotten Son, that whosoever believed in Him, should not perish from this earth." For God sent not the Son into the world to judge the world, but that the world should be saved through Him. God help me and keep me in this faith. Amen.

C. Junker.

Kelskov, June 9, 1870, (6 days later).

Today, Friday, I and all our traveling companions partook in communion. May God bless that for us.

June 10, 1870, Saturday 6 P.M.

My parents and I have been in Nustrop to bid farewell to our dear minister, who has served us for eighteen years. He has confirmed me and I love him more than any other minister. He bade me write him a letter occasionally and that I promised to do. He bade me also to remember all the good things we so often had talked about. May the Lord help me that I never forget. God bless both him and me and if it should be His will, I should be very happy to meet and talk with him again, but if not, God help us that we may meet in heaven, where we never shall part. The Lord

be with us. This will probably be the last I'll write in my
home land.

Hamborg, Germany, Sunday June 12, 1870, 9:30 A.M. (3
days later)
    We arrived at Voyeus, having parted with all our relatives
and dear friends, who were very heavy hearted at our depar-
ture. We have already seen a great deal on our trip to this
place Hamborg, and the scenery is beautiful. At noon we
came through Flensborg, but didn't see a great deal of the
city, the railroad didn't go through there. We then came
to Slevig where we saw the Gottorp Slot Castle and the
sea surrounding it and there we saw the Danish Vold Dan-
nevirke, which for a long time has been a protection around
Denmark and Germany. Then we came to Rendelborg which
also was a beautiful place, but the most beautiful of all was
Prinsborg, where there was such beautiful woods, parks with
so many beautiful trees, and parks that one could never
get tired of looking at them and walking around in them
as the people who lived there do everyday. The next place
was Altona, but then we didn't leave the train and from
there we came back to Hamborg. We rode underground
3 or 4 different places. As soon as we got off the train
the officials met us and took us to our stopping place at
C. Meirs, where we are to stay until Wednesday, when we
start across the big ocean. We have had coffee here once
and were served so much we could hardly drink it all. Now
it's nearly evening so I shall not write any more today.
                                                        C. Junker.


Hamborg, June 13, 1870.
    We slept well last night although the beds were hard
and the bedding scarce. All it consisted of was one mattress
and one quilt. This morning we took in the town. First we
were in No. 33, 39 Amerathtukrase. After that we went
through Saint Niccloi Church, which was beautiful. I have
never seen anything so majestic. The pulpit was made of
marble, as was the baptismal fount. The chairs and seats
were over-stuffed. This church burned down in the big fire
of 1842 and is still in the process of rebuilding. The tower
is only half finished and it already reaches way above the

house tops, even those that are seven stories high. After we left the church we saw a large funeral procession. The horses on the hearse were covered with black robes and were led by two men dressed in black. Following the hearse walked the pall-bearers and two carriages came later. We then went for dinner and had peas and pork and it tasted good. At four o'clock we had coffee but no cake only what we ourselves had brought along. At 6:30 we had supper and a little later on coffee. Then we went to bed.

Caroline Junker.


Hamborg, June 14, 1870

This morning our trunks were taken down to the ship and my father and Jens went along down to the ship. Then came inspection and this afternoon we have run all over town trying on shoes, finally we found some that would do. Then we went to gather up our things, for tomorrow we sail.

Caroline Junker.


Wednesday, June 15, 1870

We walked all the way to the dock and became very tired. We then entered a launch that took us out to the ocean liner Allemanice. When we entered the ship we were taken to the middle deck, here we were so closely packed it became almost unbearable. Our eats are not bad, but the ship rocks, one becomes dizzy and loses ones appetite. I didn't sleep well the first night, but perhaps it will be better.


Thursday, June 16, 1870

When we got up this morning, Anna and I were very ill. This feeling left us when we got up on deck and Jens brought us some ham and mustard that we'd brought with us from home. We remained up on deck all day, except at meal times. At eventide we saw a light house on the coast of England. I have often longed to see this country (England), as well as to sail on the ocean, now I've had my wishes granted, but it is not as I expected it to be. Is anything what we expect?

Friday, June 17, 1870

This morning I could see land from where I lay in bed. This is France, the coast was rock bound. For some reason the ship lay quietly for quite some time. When we did sail the wind blew so hard the ship rolled heavily. Just as the dinner gong sounded we landed in LaHavre, France, and we are told that we shall not set sail until tomorrow noon. A ladder was lowered and we went ashore. Now we both saw and heard the French, as this place is a large harbor full of sailing vessels both large and small. The city itself we hardly saw for we dare not wander far. We see a number of things hewn out of stone, but we have not the slightest idea what they are used for. We returned to the ship just as the tea bell rang. Many French ladies have visited the ship, some merely for curiosity, but a few are making the trip with us. Now the passengers are dancing to their heart's content whenever the weather is fit. We are going to bed soon.

Wednesday, June 22, 1870, 6 P.M. (5 days later)

I hope now that it won't be long until we see land. For over a week we've seen nothing but water and during all this time I've been bed fast with seasickness. One could never imagine how terrible that can be. This afternoon we've sighted land which we hope is the long anticipated land of America.

July 1, 1870, New York (9 days later)

This afternoon at five we entered the city of New York. We anchored the 29th of June. From the Allemanice (the ocean liner) we boarded a smaller boat which took us into New York. We have seen very little of the city yet, but what we have seen is magnificent. We are lodged in a Danish hotel, by the name of Scandinavian. Quite a change has come over ones appetite since leaving the ship.

                                                            Caroline.

New York, June 3, 1870 (3 days later)

We have been here now for three days but will soon be on our way by train to Sioux City in the State of Iowa. It will be a five days journey with the flyer. Yesterday we took in the sights of the city, New York. But the grandeur of what we saw defies description. The streets are approximately sixteen miles in length. There was a park, where several wild animals were kept, and where also were beautiful lakes. Also two water fountains made of gold, in such a way that as it arose the water looked golden. Our lodging for these three days cost fifteen dollars. Today I wrote two letters home, the first I've written from America.

July 6, 1870 (3 days later)

On the train between Chicago and Sioux City everything was so green and so beautiful that we were simply entranced. Of course it was all so new to us, but never the less I have never seen anything more beautiful. Along in the night we arrived at a city called Harrisburg. Here the train stopped for a couple of hours, then off and away again, all that night and three days following. The first state we crossed was New York, where everything was grand, beautiful homes, fruitful fields and many orchards laden with fruit of all kinds. The next State was Pennsylvania. Here we found large mountain ranges covered with forests. Not as many cities as New York. Homes are more scattered and much of the land not cultivated.

A number of places the train went under ground and other places the train went right along the edge of the cliffs. The valleys were so deep one got quite dizzy looking down at them. In this state we stopped at a place named Pittsburg, where we changed trains. The next state we got into was Illinois, which was more beautiful than Pennsylvania. There the land is flat and again we saw large fields of corn and grain.

When we got to Chicago we had all our belongings taken out to the Western depot where we got on to another train, that was to take us to Sioux City. We got there at noon the following day. Here we met a Swede who took us to a hotel where we had our dinner served American style. We had steak, potatoes, rice, jelly, currants, sweet pudding, several kinds of sauce, ice water and sweet cake. When we had finished our dinner we were taken to our room. The floors were covered with carpets. We didn't stay here very long. We rented two rooms where we could stay until our agent came back. Jens and Johannes went along with a

Norwegian family away up into Dakota and then they walked
to Lincoln (now Meckling). Here there lived a Danish family
they knew in Denmark. They then drove forty-five miles
to Sioux City after us. We stayed in the home of a Norwegian
mid-wife. She was a very nice lady and we could easily understand her language. It was a Monday afternoon that we left
Sioux City with a big load. The men had to walk.

We drove about five miles that day. We camped that
night in the woods just across the woods from the big Sioux
river. The next morning we broke camp very early so we
didn't notice the heat so much. At noon we camped right
under the open skies near a city called Elk Point. It is called
a city but it isn't as large as one of our little villages in
Denmark. We rested here a couple of hours, then we drove
until sundown. The air was very warm and it lightened and
thundered for a couple of hours but no rains came from
it. The mosquitoes were so bad we hardly slept at all and
when we awoke we were full of red spots on both hands
and face, where they had stung us. Yesterday July 13, we
drove thirty miles but we still have thirteen miles to go.
It will be late before we arrive at our destination since the
man folks have some business to see while we are in
Vermillion.

Vermillion, July 14, 1870, Thursday.

Things didn't turn out for me the way I had expected.
I didn't get to go along to Clay County. Just as I was waiting,
a man from the hotel in Vermillion rode out to where we
were camping. He wanted a girl to work, so I took the job.
In a hurry I got my things sorted out and went back to
Vermillion with him. There is a Norwegian girl working here
and she helps me a lot, especially in explaining to me what
I am expected to do since I don't understand the English
language. [This girl later became Mrs. O. B. Larson and
after they were married they lived just one mile apart all
the rest of their lives.] The work doesn't seem so hard and
every afternoon I have two hours to myself. We get up at
five o'clock in the morning and help with the kitchen work
until every one has eaten, then we wash dishes, a girl who
I think is the daughter and myself. After that we make
the beds then back to the kitchen to help there until dinner

is over. Then washing dishes again the same as in the morning, and again in the evening. It is quite different and the work is not as hard as in Denmark. If only I had known the language, that's the hardest of all. Now I must go and help with the supper again.

C. Junker.

Monday, July 18, 1870.

Last Friday I wrote the first letter to my parents that I have ever written to them and now I am looking for them to come to town any day. Yesterday, Sunday I surely was lonesome for them and for Denmark. I thought many times I had gone to Nustrop church and listened to Provost Bladel preach. Yesterday was the fifth Sunday since I have been to church. Last evening a Norwegian girl, who had been home to see her parents came here. She works for an American lady. Since there wasn't room for her to sleep upstairs she slept with me. We went to bed before the rest of the folks did. She asked me what Faith I belonged to, I told her I believed in the Tribune God: Father, Son and Holy Ghost. She had the same faith. After that she said a prayer out loud and I have never heard one more beautiful and sincere. I believe God will help me that I too may be sincere in my prayers for myself and those I love. Amen.

Thursday, July 21, 1870 (3 days later)

Today I left Vermillion. My father came after me. I received two dollars for the week I had spent here, but from now on the lady would only pay $1.50 a week and for those wages I wouldn't stay, so I came here with my father and I am still staying, though I don't like it here. [They lived in part of someone's barn and this is the reason we think she did not like it.] We are anxiously waiting for father and Jens to come from their wanderings in search of land. Last Sunday we went to church. This church is about six miles back towards Vermillion. The minister is Norwegian, but we could readily understand him. The ritual was the same as back in Denmark. Communion too was held this day.

Wednesday, August 17, 1870 (3 weeks later)

For a whole week now I've been working for an American farmer where I get two dollars a week. It is mostly for the sake of learning the American language that I came here. If I had only known that, time would go faster.

Sunday, August 21, 1870

Today my youngest sister was confirmed by a Norwegian minister who lives just a mile from here. He is a very nice man and he preached a very good sermon, as good a sermon as any of our ministers back home could have done. Now if only she and all the rest of us heed the advice and admonition he gave us. God help us that we may have need of no fear and may God help my sister that she remains faithful to the pact she entered into today.

C. Junker.

February 23, 1871.

Weeks and months have now passed since I last wrote in this book and many things have changed since then. We are now, not on the same place but not very far from that former place, where we lived in a barn, just a quarter of a mile from here. There has been a great change. We now own our own house and home and together with that God has given us better health which is the best of all. I had worked at the same place for three months, when I came home for a short while. I had only been home three weeks, when one Sunday just as my brother Jens and I came home from church, we had been to communion too, came two men from Yankton, that were looking for a girl. I got ready and went with them. I got to work at a hotel and received three dollars a week. I did not like the place very well. I had been at this place only five weeks when my oldest brother who had just come back from Michigan came to see me and I came home with him and ever since then I have stayed at home. People say that the Dakota winters are very severe, but to date the weather has been most pleasant. We've had a few weeks of cold weather, but they were soon followed by the most pleasant and agreeable days. But perhaps we may experience some real winter yet since February is only half gone.

Today one of our travelling companions, Jens Skroder has taken a claim above Yankton. He became very angry, and had no reason to get angry with my father when he bought his property. He himself had said he wanted to stay around here until his children were older, but father did not want to wait for that, so bought land here. We go to visit Anna, the wife, occasionally, when he is not at home, and she and her brother with her children likewise come to see us now and then, when he is not at home. This man Jens Skroder had a habit of leaving home and staying away days at a time.

We have had several letters from Denmark lately. The other day we had one from our neighbor Paulsen who wrote that our old home burned down and now lay in ruins. This made us very sad even though we are a long ways from there now. Little did we think when we built it five or six years ago that it so soon would change into a heap of ashes. But thank God it didn't happen while we lived there. We at least can't see it now. We can only imagine how bare and dreary it must look. He also wrote that as far as neighbors went, they hadn't made a very good trade, meaning the people that now lived on our place, and it made us very happy to know that they still think of us with pleasure and are happy to hear from us, their dear friends who now have been in this Great America for quite some time.

Caroline Junker.

# "Nursed During the Civil War with Clara Barton; Was a Charter Member of the Red Cross" Maria Anne Nesbitt Walworth County 1883

by Mrs. A. W. Davidson

Maria Anne Nesbitt was born March 17, 1831, on a large plantation in Virginia, Occomac County, near the Wagram Pond P.O. She was the fourth child of William Walker Nesbitt and Margaret Elizabeth Nesbitt (nee Smith). Both her father and mother were of pre-revolutionary families of Scotch Irish descent.

William Nesbitt also owned property in Indiana County, Pennsylvania. Robert, the eldest son, was sent north to administer this property.

When Maria was ten a baby sister was born, christened Margaret. The gentle mother died. In a few years Maria had finished the education considered necessary at the time for southern gentlewomen, and begged to go forth to live with Robert and his wife in Pennsylvania. Beset with the cares of his motherless household and wishing to remarry, her father gave his consent the more readily, as he knew with what poor grace Maria would accept a stepmother, and he realized that this restless daughter would never conform to the pattern set for southern girls of that time. The girl wanted to study Greek and Latin! The aunts tsked-tsked and William shook his head.

Life in Pennsylvania was a dream come true for Maria. Happily she matriculated and was graduated from the Seminary at Pittsburgh without the hateful stigma of "blue stocking." For ten years following her graduation she taught in Pittsburgh and adjacent towns, returning every summer for post graduate work at the Seminary. In the meantime her brother James, two years her senior, and her favorite, had like so many venturesome young men made the long hazardous trip to the gold fields in California in '49 and returned to take Robert's place in the business in Pennsylvania.

James married a Pennsylvania girl and settled in Indiana County. Robert and his family returned to Virginia, having always felt alien in the North.

With the opening gun of the Civil War, the Nesbitt family was split with a bitter feud. James and Maria in the North, and Robert and William in the South. James was elected Captain of a company of Pennsylvania volunteers and William and Robert were Confederate officers. Maria was at this time thirty years old and by the concepts of that time an old maid. Still, in 1860 she became betrothed to a young doctor, John Wilson, who established a practice in Youngstown. John Wilson enlisted in the same company of volunteers as her brother James. During the winter of 1861-62, both men came home on furlough – a short time and joyous period for the family.

In August of 1862, the casualty lists following the second battle of Bull Run carried the names, Nesbitt – James S., Cap't., missing in action; Wilson, John M.O., killed in action. In the days and weeks that followed, the revised lists read: Nesbitt, James S., Cap't., missing, believed captured.

Putting aside her own grief to comfort James' young wife, who was expecting her second baby, Maria decided to make the trip to Virginia to enlist the aid of relatives, to find her brother. It was a difficult journey that ended in disappointment, for there was no record found of James in any southern prison.

Despite the combined efforts of her family to persuade her to stay (indeed, she found that they considered her in the light of a prodigal returned to the fold) she returned to Pennsylvania. In the meantime, word had come that Captain Nesbitt was seriously wounded and had been transferred to one of the hospital boats. Again Maria set out, this time to Washington. There, for anxious weeks, she sought some news of James to no avail. The capital was crammed with people on the same sad errand. Hearing of a band of women volunteer nurses, who were to go south through the blockade, she used every bit of influence she could bring to bear to contact their leader, Clara Barton. Miss Barton's interest and sympathy were aroused and Maria enlisted as a nurse. The following months were a story of hard, unremitting toil and hardship. The one bright spot was that she did find James, wasted by fever, and with a desperate hip wound, but alive. In later years she declared that the most disagreeable part of her whole nursing experience was the reek of boiled cabbage that hung about the hospital ships!

Following the War, she returned to the teaching profession, and in 1875, she received her life certificate.

She was deeply interested in the Red Cross organized by Clara Barton in 1881, and she was a charter member. She traveled through the Eastern states in the summer of 1881-82 in the interests of that organization.

In the meantime, she lived with her brother, his wife, and their ten children. When the eldest two boys of the family came to Dakota territory in 1882, she followed in the summer of '83 to see that they were properly fed and cared for. In 1884 she filed on a homestead adjoining theirs. The country abounded with wild game, deer, prairie chickens, ducks and geese. Miss Maria's first project after her arrival was a vegetable garden. The boys grumbled but they enjoyed the bountiful meals and so did the other young hungry bachelor homesteaders who began to drop in casually, just about mealtime.

The land homesteaded by the Nesbitts was along the eastern side of the Missouri River, in Walworth County, below the present town of Mobridge. Mad Bear's camp was directly across the river.

Mad Bear was one of the Fool Soldier Indians who had sworn friendship to the white settlers. He and the members of his camp became very friendly with the Nesbitt brothers, and this friendliness was extended to Miss Maria when she came. She considered it a dubious honor, outraged at the lack of ceremony with which the Indians pushed open the door and entered at any time of the day or night. It would have disturbed this staid maiden lady to know that the Indians considered her the boy's mother, even though they called her "Aunt!" Among certain tribes of the Sioux, "Uncle," and sometimes "Aunt," are purely titles of respect. For many years Maria did not know that the whole Indian camp called her "Aunt," as the boys gravely assured her it was an Indian name and meant "Black Arrow." The young men friends of the Nesbitt boys, in on the secret, insisted that it meant "Breadmaker," and, indeed, the heavenly aroma of the golden brown crusty loaves that Miss Maria turned out on baking day, drew the appreciation of the whites and Indians alike.

She was an expert cook and proud of it and it pleased her when Mad Bear, with great ceremony, requested that she teach a few chosen young women the art of making the "Rising Bread." This she did. Any form of teaching found her in her own element, and although only Maggie Mad Bear spoke or understood English, it was Miss Maria's firm conviction that she could make the girls understand if she spoke slowly and carefully. Strangely enough, the results sustained her belief.

Firmly she instilled the idea that the first part of the recipe for bread was a meticulous scrubbing of the hands! Sternly she banished her own nephews and their friends from these sessions, finding that their presence would completely demoralize her class, who either hid or giggled ceaselessly with their eyes downcast.

In the meantime, the new little town of Bangor was established and after that Miss Maria spent a part of each winter there. She taught two or three terms of school there, and also taught in the Presbyterian Sunday School.

She made a visit each year back to Pennsylvania and Virginia and her enthusiastic accounts of Dakota brought James and his wife out to file on land along the river. They stayed but a short time, however, and sold their land to a son. Later she brought her niece Annie Nesbitt back to Dakota with her. Annie also taught school in Bangor and Evarts. She married Mark Glerup and they made their home in Evarts.

Miss Maria was a charter member of the Women's Relief Corps, organized in Bangor, and at the initial meeting, read a letter from Miss Clara Barton with whom she had kept up a correspondence since Civil War days. At that time, 1898, Miss Barton was in the Philippines establishing a field hospital at the age of 78.

Maria, with Scotch thrift, had put aside enough of her salary through the years to accumulate a nice little nest egg. True, her salary was much better than that of most women teachers. Those summer sessions were bearing fruit. A former pupil, James D. Swain, a man of wealth and with far-flung business interests, invested her small capital so that she received a substantial income, making her financially independent, a great advantage at any age, but especially at a time when so many lines of work were closed to women.

She traveled a great deal, usually taking one of her numerous nieces or nephews with her. A host of friends, among them many former pupils from north, south, east, and west, welcomed a visit from this erect, handsome, elderly lady with her deep sense of humor and pungent wit. She was famed as a brilliant conversationalist, no doubt in part, because she was also an intent and ready listener!

In the years between 1900-1914, Miss Maria divided her time in the homes of several nieces and nephews. In her later years her chief pleasure was in the letters she received from her own relations, as well as numbers of former pupils who wrote her from all over the world. These she answered promptly. She was alert and active, interested in world affairs until the last week of her life. In 1914, she passed away at 83 years of age, following a stroke, at the home of a nephew, William H. Nesbitt, in Lemmon, South Dakota. She is buried in the Lemmon cemetery where a simple stone marks her grave, inscribed only, Maria A. Nesbitt 1831-1914. On every Memorial Day a squad of Boy Scouts drop a wreath of poppies on her grave and plant a flag, to honor a Civil War nurse who served her country faithfully and well.

# "The story of the wife of a Pioneer Doctor in the Rosebud Country"
## Jessie McGrath Overton
## Tripp County
## 1905

*[The ninth child of Canadian parents, Jessie was born in Dallas Center County, Iowa in 1880. She attended St. Patricks Parochial School in Danbury, Iowa, a small town just south of Sioux City.]*

I was always busy doing things for the sisters, and spent most of my time taking music lessons. I just loved to run errands for the nuns at St. Patricks school. When I was quite young I played for the choir at St. Patrick's church, and most everything that came along that had to have organ music. My brothers played for all the dances in the community, and every now and then I would go along with them.

I started to teach in Woodbury County and went to Morningside Teachers College to get a teachers certificate, then taught till my certificate ran out. Then went to Fremont Teachers College in Nebraska to renew my teaching certificate. This went on every summer until I quit teaching.

My oldest brother Tom was a good friend of Father McNamara in Bloomfield, Nebraska. Father wanted some one to direct a choir, so Tom told his priest about me, and I heard from Father McNamara right away. He told me if I would come to Bloomfield to direct the choir, he would see to it that I got a class of music students. That really did appeal to me. So I went out to the Bloomfield country all excited with the idea of pioneering. When I got to their town, Father McNamara had a very good friend who used to play Chess with him. He was the Bloomfield's new young handsome doctor. I met the Chess player and in due time we were married. Our wedding date was October 18th, 1904.

That fall the Republicans had some kind of excursion to Yankton. Each ticket sold had a number on it, and this

103

number might be one of the lucky ones to draw a homestead in South Dakota, in Gregory County. Well, Dr. Overton was one of the lucky ones. I was against it all the time, but I could see that he did intend to go to South Dakota, even though he was warned that there wasn't anything out in that part of the country but Indians and babies. That is what did it I guess. He thought that was the place for a young doctor.

We were supposed to be on the homestead by February 1, 1905, but due to very severe winter the government extended the time till May 1. The first of February came along, the snow and cold weather were too much to take, so we stayed in our nice home till in the spring.

In preparation for the trip Doctor bought a team of broncos, Bird and Betsy, and had a covered wagon made out of a heavy spring wagon. One of our Bloomfield friends gave us a spotted bird dog. Then we were ready for the long trip to Dixon, South Dakota. It proved to be a long trip, too. One whole week, rained most of the way, and finally we had to stop in Moniowi, Nebraska because the roads got too heavy for our team. We stayed there two days, and I cried most every minute we were there. I was so lonesome for our friends in Bloomfield and our nice little home we left behind. Finally the weather changed and we were on our way again.

There were no roads on the section lines then so we approached Dixon on an angling road from the southeast. As we approached the town we could see a large building coming into town from the northwest. We learned it was to be the Dixon General Store that was to be placed on the street of Dixon. Everyone was so glad to see us, you would think we knew everyone there. They were especially glad to see dad for there was a sick little girl in town. They were homesteaders too, and were on their way to another location. I just can't remember where they were going. The little girl was quite sick too, but got along just fine and the people were on their way in a few days. It was dad's first sick call in the Rosebud Country. I will never forget the wonderful supper we had that night in the Covered Wagon cafe in Dixon. The best fried potatoes and baking powder biscuits that would just melt in your mouth.

Our Homestead Days were very happy ones. Each year seemed to bring more happiness than the year before. All we had when we arrived was a covered wagon, team of horses, spotted bird dog and a partly built dugout for a home. The day after we arrived we went out to our dugout to complete it. Our neighbors had arrived and were waiting for us. They lived just across the section line from our section. We then lived a half-mile east and a half-mile north of Dixon. Our road was diagonal across the section, so it wasn't so far then. Our dug-out was a hole in the ground about four feet deep. It had a frame building of about three feet on top on this hole. The roof wasn't too good. Every time it rained the water came in on us. We had to fix strings of cloth from the leak in the roof to a pan so the water would run down the string. This kept the rain off of us. We didn't have much room, but this was our palace.

We had so much company that first summer. All our friends were so curious to see the kind of life we were living. And what fun we had entertaining them. We stayed in this dugout till late in the fall and moved in a big hurry one day. I was sitting on a step coming down into our home. I got up to talk to dad or to do something, when a snake fell right on the step I had just left. That was the day we moved into our new sod house. The snakes were coming in out of the cold.

Our bird dog made many friends for us. We didn't hunt at all, for dad couldn't hit the broad side of the barn, but we got our share of birds caught, just for the use of our dog. The Dixon Country is, and always will be, the garden spot of the world for me. We had so many good times, so many friends, and some of them are still there yet.

After we moved into the sod house, Berniece came along very soon. This was our dream house. It had two rooms, and quite large too. We just had one party after another it seemed. The company would come, unannounced sometimes, move out all the furniture and the party was on. I had a piano in Bloomfield, for I was a music teacher back there. There was different kinds of music: piano, fiddle and just plain good singing by the group. It just seems to me that we were always doing something, or going some place all the time. Dad always had to have a good team for it was important for him to get to his patient's home in a hurry most of the time. He always had to race with the stork it seemed. There were lots of babies then for most of the people were young and having their families. A good percent were honeymooners just as dad and I were.

One time Betsy, one of the horses, got caught in a wire as dad was going across the fence. He had to do this a lot of the time. There seemed to be snow drifts, or mud puddles along the road. Sometimes he would just cut the wire and drive right over the drift. The next day that particular homesteader would know that dad had been along, and would go out and mend the fence and would report back at home that such and such a baby must have arrived, for their fence was cut. They knew the doctor had been along in the night. Getting back to Betsy, her leg was cut quite badly. Dad couldn't wait for the leg to heal so he bought another horse to team up with Bird. Her name was Nell. I got Betsy. We bought a buggy for one horse and then I was ready to work the roads. I have always had the name of being a gadabout, and I still do like to go at the drop of a hat. Betsy was quite a lively horse and loved to run with all her might. It took all the strength I had to hold her in. I traveled all over the country, down to Gregory, Dallas and even as far away as Winner. I would take my bread that was to be baked or my washing and go over to the neighbors in my new buggy. It seemed it was more fun to have some one help with the work. On my way over to the neighbor's home I would stop and pick up another friend and we would have a regular get together before the day was over. What fun!!!!

When we came to the Rosebud country I was afraid of my shadow. I would get up no matter what time of night and go with Dr. on a sick call so I wouldn't have to be alone. One night in particular I remember when I went with him. After we got to the patient's house I was afraid to stay in the buggy alone, so dad took me in with him. The Indians gave me the only stool they had to sit on. I got up just as close to dad as I could and not be in his way. I was watching every move the Indians made. They were sitting around the room smoking a pipe. During the course of the time a bug fell on my shoulder. One of the Indians reached over and brushed it off. I jumped about a foot from the stool and gave a wild yip. Every now and then one of the Indians would jump and give the same kind of yip I did and every one would laugh again. I couldn't see the funny side of this at all. After we got out of the house dad complimented me on being such a good entertainer.

In 1909 we started to build a new frame house. It took us quite a while to get it done. The plan of the house was taken from Dr. Overton's old home in Nebraska City where he was raised. By spring of 1910 we were in this house and Claire, our second child, was born. I remember of having company one day. I had placed the baby on the bed in her best show off clothes. When the company came, of course the baby was on parade. The first guests went in to see her and there on her dress was a bed bug. At first it was quite serious but we soon laughed that off.

Our big moment was when we bought our Brush car. I believe there were five different people around Dixon that bought a Brush at the same time. We would race with the neighbors who had horses on our way to Gregory to a baseball game. On the way down the hill we would be ahead. Then on the way up the hill the team would be ahead. One day I was going out in the county with dad in the Brush car. This car had no windshield. I had a large hat on, and tied with a large auto veil so it wouldn't blow off of my head. At that time I wore a duster coat with large sleeves. This was the Vogue. I had to hold onto my hat even with the veil. We were driving along very nicely when zing!! a bird flew in to the sleeve of my coat. I jumped up, threw my arms around, the large sleeves blew in front of dad which almost caused an auto accident. Today it would have caused a huge accident. We had a good laugh after it was all over with.

We stayed in Dixon for nineteen years and moved to Winner in the summer of 1921. It was about time for the two older girls to go to high school, so we thought it wise to move where there would be good schools. All the children went to the Winner schools, then on to college.

Our intentions were to just stay for the eight months to prove up on the homestead. We would move right back to Bloomfield the minute that time was up. Here I am, still in this country fifty-four years from that May 1, 1904.

My roots have grown deep in the Rosebud country. I am sure if I had to move elsewhere I would be just like I was when we moved from Bloomfield, Nebraska. I would shed many tears. But I expect if I have to move, it will be just as it was before. There are always many good people most any place you might move to.

# Daisy Herpel Potter
# Day County
# 1882

Reprinted from the *Reporter and Farmer,* Webster, South Dakota
June 11, 1931

My parents, Mr. and Mrs. J. C. Herpel, came to Andover
from Michigan in the fall of '82. After suffering several hemor-
rhages of the lungs, my father was advised by physicians
to seek a dryer climate, and like many others of that time,
went west in the hope of a cure. Still weak and sick upon
arrival, he was for some time confined to his bed in the
hotel, and this story is told of his experience there. His room
in this hastily built structure was directly above the office,
from which his constant coughing could be plainly heard.
One afternoon a group of men were sitting around the office.
Upon hearing the familiar coughing in the room above, the
Doctor remarked, "Well, there's a man that came out here
to die, and we're going to have a funeral here some of these
days." "And where shall we hold it?" asked the minister.
Different places were suggested, none of which seemed
adequate, until it was finally decided, at the suggestion of
the section boss, that they hold it in the depot. "And do
you know," remarked the lawyer, "that we haven't a cemetery."
So they got out the plat of the town and laid out a place
for the cemetery. All of this time utterly unconscious of
the fact that if they could hear him cough, he could hear
them talk, and as he later remarked, "It isn't often one has
the opportunity of hearing his funeral so fully discussed."
At any rate the plans were laid aside, and to make a long
story short, or rather to make a short story long for it did
take a long time, he got well, and still lives at the well
seasoned age of 76, many years after the Dr. and the lawyer
and the minister have been laid to rest.

Father did manage however to file on a claim in Union Township before winter set in. I was born in town the following spring: the first [white] baby in Andover.

The story goes that some one asked "Have you seen the new baby?" "Yes," the other replied "She's a Daisy," which of course was just a slang expression of the day, and had no particular bearing on the case. However some kind friend whose name is now lost in oblivion penned this little poem which was printed in the *Reporter and Farmer* in March, 1883. After that the folks thought it would be just the thing to name me Daisy Andover, and that I was baptized. In later years this was something of a cross for me, though I didn't say much about it, but I sort of envied the girls who had pretty names like Flora Belle, and such, but after I heard of J. Pierpont Morgan, I didn't feel so bad. [Pierpont was the name of the nearest town.]

### *Daisy of Andover*

*This morning there's joy in our little town,*
*This morn at the breaking of day,*
*For a wee little stranger has knocked at our gate,*
*And claims our permission to stay.*

*Tis a sweet little woman, a wee little maid,*
*That has crept to our arms and our hearts,*
*And we gladly received her, and loved her at once,*
*And we hope she may never depart.*

*Tis the first little babe that has come to our town.*
*And may life full of pleasure and grace,*
*Ever smile on our darling, our beautiful babe,*
*And bring joy to her sweet bonny face.*

*And may the fleet years as they journey along,*
*Bring nothing but joy to the life.*
*Of Daisy of Andover, God's gift of love,*
*To our friends J. C. Herpel and wife.*

I never remember having lived on the homestead as my parents moved later to a preemption which they procured on the south edge of town. Here we resided for many years.

Our family consisting of father, mother, my sister Katha, three years older than myself, my sister Eva, better known as Bobby, who was two years younger than I, and myself.

There was a fairly good sod shanty on the place south of town which the folks later replaced with a frame house. As I look back over the years my earliest recollections center about the sod house. It was papered in newspapers but was later redone in real wall paper with lovely blue roses on it. One end of the main room was fixed up for a bed room, and the other for a kitchen. There was also a lean-to on the west where we girls slept, three in a bed. Another lean-to on the east, served as back shed and summer kitchen. We also enjoyed a splendid well of water that came nearly to the top of the ground.

We girls walked back and forth to school in town, which then consisted of a wooden structure with one room upstairs and another down.

The artesian well which was one of the finest in the state, was a matter of considerable pride to the little village of Andover, especially since Groton had a muddy one. For besides supplying the town, the overflow was piped out to the end of Main Street into a large artificial lake. The fountain that fed this was a constant delight to us children, we loved to watch it throw its stream of crystal water 15 or 20 feet in the air, running day and night, winter and summer. The lake was supplied with several row boats which afforded many an evening's enjoyment for the young people round about. Skating was enjoyed in winter.

The powerful water pressure afforded fire protection also, the hose throwing water to the top of the highest elevator. I remember one day they were trying out the fire hose on Main street, then one of the men took it to flush off the side walk in front of his place of business. Another man came along, he was dressed in the latest fashion of that time. They had some disagreement, one hasty word followed another, the man with the hose turned it directly on the other. Bystanders fled to cover, I ducked into Bob Martyn's tailor shop, from which point of vantage I was an eye witness to this juicy bit of scandal, and can remember yet the half drowned man standing there, the water gushing in rivers from the beautifully tailored legs. I often think how well the men dressed in those days and can well remember [them] coming down the teetery board sidewalk to church of a Sunday morning dressed in Prince Albert coats, high silk hats, gray trousers, kid gloves and walking sticks.

Who could ever forget the annual Sunday School picnic often held at Lynn Lake? I noticed in the paper just the other day that the Seniors of the Andover High School went out for a little outing. They stopped off at Lake Kampeska, from there they went to Roslyn to a ball game, from there they went to Aberdeen and took in a show. I wonder what they would think of sitting on boards across the box of a lumber wagon, in the broiling sun behind a slow team, over grass roads headed for Lynn Lake.

Yet how eagerly we looked forward to this important event. After scarcely sleeping the night before in excited anticipation, we rose early the next morning, fed and watered the calves and chickens, picketed out the cows, and left everything in as good shape as possible. Finished packing the lunches, then for a good scrub, and braid up the pig tails for each other, and don the brand new pink sunbonnets, and join the train of wagons headed for the cool and shady shores of Lynn Lake. I can still remember how stiff and tired we got, and oh, so hungry after our early and hurried breakfast. But when we piled out of these hot and dusty wagons, into the long cool grass under those lovely trees, it seemed that Heaven itself could hold no added joy.

How we scampered about, while the men carried water and the women unpacked the lunches, and made the lemonade, that inevitable accompaniment to every well regulated picnic. Meanwhile Mr. Carpenter got out the big coil of new rope he always brought along, and soon had several fine swings in working order. While this was going on Ed Putman the town bachelor and descendant of the famous Israel of Revolutionary days, got busy with his sharp and trusty jack knife, and made willow whistles for all the boys and girls. In fact he never let up till every child had one. When the call to dinner came, how we fell to, and such an array of goodies! After eating our fill, then came the long afternoon of swinging, games, and rollicking under those wonderful trees, for we simply had none at home, remember. Then another lunch, the horses were watered and hitched, and next came the long trek home in the cool of the evening. How hard it was to stay awake on those hard boards after such a strenuous day. Then home again unloading in the dark, a few hasty chores by lantern light and bed time again. Such was the Sunday School picnic of the early days.

The first funeral I really remember, was that of little Ada Johnson, six year old daughter and only child of Mr. and Mrs. Art Johnson. "And we wept that one so lovely should have had a life so brief" for she was such a sweet little thing, with beautiful golden curls as entrancing as any Goldilocks of story book fame. Ever after that, young as I was, my heart went out to those sorrowing ones who laid their loved ones away in that barren wind-swept spot, the cemetery that was platted out, you remember.

It was but a little ways, and in full view of our house, perhaps it was a baby, or some poor mother, who had given up her life that another might live, or maybe the father of a family, who left his little brood, strangers in a strange land; we children would steal over the next day and smooth down the yellow clay, as best we could, outline the grave with rocks, or perhaps ornament it with a cross or heart done in pretty pebbles, or make a wreath of flowers, those yellow ones so common on the prairies.

The first prairie fire I remember was when I was about six and was not an important one but gave us something of a scare. My little sister was playing with her dolls in the back kitchen when she called, "Mama see the pretty, pretty." Mother was busy in the other room, and thinking it was only her doll, she said, "yes, that's nice." But she persisted and finally said, "Mama come see the pretty, pretty right now." So she dropped her work and came at once. To her surprise she saw the fire, some little distance off but coming right that way. It was early spring and there was a bare potato patch just south of the house, which sat on slightly rising ground concealing the fire from view of the town. Seizing her sunbonnet, as father was away, and charging us not to leave the house till she got back, she ran all the way to town, and spread the alarm. Soon about twenty men were on the scene. Each had taken a new broom from Wilson's store and dipped it in the lake as they passed by and rushed on to beat out the fire. I think some neighbor

plowed a furrow with a walking plow. We watched them
straggling back several hours later tired and smoked up,
the brooms smoked black, the fire out.

The first wedding that it was my privilege to witness
was that of my aunt Miss Anna Ellis to Louis J. Gower.
This was solemnized in the new house, which had been
embellished with new ingrain carpet in the parlor and best
bed room, new curtains and sofa, a fine Art Garland stove
and an oak center table with two shelves for the albums.
The guests included but a few intimate friends and as we
had no relatives here the company was a small one. How
sweet and womanly my aunt looked, in her well fitting gown
of brown taffeta with the cream silk lace at the throat. Why
did they all weep, and the supper, that was the main thing
I thought.

The first Christmas I can remember was in the old Mills
hall, but before that they had them in the depot. There was
a big tree loaded with pretty things. My sister and I each
got a bottle of Hoight's German Cologne and a big doll with
a china head and as well set a permanent as one would
wish to see. Subsequent Christmases, mostly in the Methodist
Church, were equally delightful. I don't think we ever missed
one no matter how deep the snow or how cold the night,
father saw to that. Snuggled down in the hay in the home
made sleigh with plenty of blankets and the old buffalo robe
the short distance we had to go took but a few minutes,
and the effort was well repaid.

The first blizzard I remember was the famous one of
'88. We were still living in the sod and I distinctly recall
that a friend who batched it on a claim many miles to the
south stopped with us when the storm came on. He and
father took down the clothes line and tied it about the waist
of one of them, while they held the end of it at the back
door. Thus they brought in coal and water and did the chores,
making things snug and tight. I even remember them pour-
ing many pails of water over the shanty roof, where it froze
in an icy sheet that kept out the bitter wind as well as
snow that might have sifted in. We could scarcely tell when
the storm was over as the snow was packed completely over
the sod shanty so that every window was a blank wall. When
the wind finally went down, the next day I suppose, they

opened up the back door which luckily opened in, and there was the pattern of the door in the snow clear to the top, a neat white wall. After filling the wash boiler and tubs with snow, the men cut steps up and out for the snow was so hard it would hold up the weight of a man.

Another thing I remember so well was the barrels of apples that came from Michigan, what bright spots they were in a fruitless land. First the letter saying that one had been sent, then the weeks of waiting till the happy day arrived, when father brought it home from the depot. How we gathered around when it was opened, oh, how good it smelled. If Grandma Herpel sent it, in the top would be a big package of home knit stockings and mittens. What a world of work they must have been! No one was forgotten, each was a size larger than the year before. Then farther down in the barrel was the usual flour sack of home dried apples for pies, and in the bottom the sack of black walnuts. If it were from Grandma Ellis, stowed away in the middle was a can of maple sugar, and a sack of butternuts or perhaps a stone jar of apple butter or blackberry jam sealed tight with rosin and beeswax. And the apples, how good they tasted, the greasy Pippins, the golden Bell Flower, the Rambos, the Northern Spys, and the Tolman Sweets. How good these mothers were to go to all this work for us. One a foster mother, the other a step-mother with a large brood of her own still at home, for both our parents had lost their mothers at an early age.

Though we never suffered the real privations that fell the lot of some, I often marveled later that mother always found the money somewhere, for a few good books and the best of magazines and always the daily paper from Chicago or Minneapolis. Many a Sunday afternoon she spent reading aloud to the family, and father, realizing our restrictions and being an orphan in his childhood, was so good to take us with him whenever he could and painstakingly showed us many points of interest. I even remember his taking me to Minneapolis on a business trip when I was only four and I still recall many things that happened, perhaps because we were blockaded and spent two weeks on the train. I was the only child along and came in for lots of attention, and no doubt came back badly spoiled. Another time he took

my sister and me to Michigan to visit at the old home and
treated us to several days of sightseeing in Minneapolis and
Chicago.

A narration of this sort would be incomplete without
a reference to our pony, a red and white spotted bronco
named Dan, and a real cow pony of the old school, having
been trained on a big cattle ranch out west. At any rate
he certainly knew his stuff, and his splendid training often
made up for my inexperience. To really do him justice would
nearly take a book. He could be guided by merely a hand
on his neck, or simply leaning to the side, and leave it to
him to head a cow for home. He could round up a bunch
of cattle and take them out to feed with no one on his back,
indeed I often saw him do it. I was only five when Reuben
Stewart taught me how to ride. My older sister was never
very strong and did not care to ride and my younger was
too small and did not ride till later. It always fell my lot
to be the cowboy of the family and do all the errands,
even some for the neighbors, for there were no cars or phone.
I'm sure old settlers remember me best in my yellow sunbonnet, tearing down the road on his back, chasing off stray
stock, or on another jaunt after old Mrs. Schrader's cow
that would run off while she was away washing.

I often wonder what life would have been to me in the
early days without that horse, for I fairly grew up with
him. Years later when I had been gone for over a year and
returned to the old home, the first thing I did was to go
down in the pasture in search of him. As soon as he saw
me coming he let out a long piercing whinny, rushed up
and nuzzled his nose against my neck. He knew me and
his welcome was complete. Could Fred Thompson have been
any prouder of Silver King?

So as I pen these lines, it all comes back to me. I can
see the miles of rolling prairie, a treeless plain, the soft green
hills to the south and east, often scarred by prairie fires,
the whirlwinds, the mirages in the quivering heat, the scattered claim shacks, the oxen and the new turned sod. I
remember the trials that fell the lot of the early settler,
the scorching wind, the prairie fire, the blizzard and the
hail, each one a story in itself. Then came the wheat, how

bright and green it looked on the nice clean sod, how beautifully it waved, changing color in the summer sun. How rich
and golden in the autumn haze, and what possibilities it
possessed: the new top buggy, a fur coat for father which
he needed badly, an organ for the parlor, and perhaps, yes
perhaps, that long hoped for trip back home.

These and many more are the memories of a little girl.

# Emily Meade Riley
## Douglas County
## 1881

### Written by Mrs. Riley in 1949

*[Born September 8, 1870 near the present city of Sleepy Eye, Minnesota, Emily was one of a family of six children whose mother was called by death in 1875. "Each of us soon learned the lesson of self-reliance," she says. Selling the last 80 acres of his preemption in 1881, her father turned most of the balance, once the $200 mortage was paid, into stock, good cows being purchased as low as $15.00 each.]*

Come with me now and see two canvas covered wagons drawn by ox teams plodding along at the rate of 20 miles per day, followed by 35 head of cattle bound for Atkinson, Nebraska, which we never reached.

The heavy snows of 1880 and 1881 reduced to water by chinook winds left mud holes a plenty. After reaching the little town of Lamberton, Minnesota, the road became only a trail. Here we camped our first night out. Rain had set in. We took refuge in a one-room abandoned cabin partly filled with corn but it afforded a better shelter than canvas.

For cooking we used a hay burning sheet iron camp stove. Bacon and eggs, homemade bread with an abundance of milk for the children and hot coffee was the menu for the first few days out. Bakeries were unknown. Crackers were often substituted for bread. These were purchased in wooden boxes of bushel capacity.

We children took turns driving cattle. This enabled us to ride in turn. The trail led us through Tracy, Tyler and Lake Benton in Minnesota. We were now in Dakota Territory and Flandreau was the first town. Sioux Falls, little more than a village, was sighted, then Marion Junction and leading down toward Scotland. Here the trail vanished completely. Headed for Niobrara and fearing we might lose our way, we stopped at a farm house to make inquiries. The owner happened to be a man who was interested in locating and surveying. He gave a glowing account of Choteau Creek Valley and persuaded the emigrants to look it over before going farther. Choteau Creek was brimful of water. Blue stem grass was more than knee high and it was ideal for stock raising and farming. The outcome was a trip to Yankton where the Federal Land Office was located. Homestead and tree claim entries were made at a filing cost of $14 each. On the return trip, lumber for the new home was bought at Scotland and hauled to the new homesite.

Well do I recall the beauty of the place that we were to call home for the next 13 years. Tall green grass and rolling prairie was everywhere. Choteau Creek, a very low banked crooked stream went winding through the valley. Buffalo bones, skulls and horns were scattered all around. Quails, prairie chickens and coyotes found a haven in the tall grass. Settlement was very sparse that summer and winter of 1881. The Joseph Lester family had come from Illinois about two weeks earlier than we and they had their little claim home built. They were standing on the opposite bank of Choteau Creek watching our ox teams pull their loads across and ready to get acquainted with their new neighbors.

In about ten days, our new house was ready for occupation. Twisted hay was fuel until the coming of the railroad in 1886. There were many lake beds full of water that, with the coming of autumn, harbored numbers of waterfowl. Gabbling, honking geese and ducks were plentiful and made choice eating.

Douglas County was fraudulently organized in February, 1891. Yankton was the territorial capital. Ordway was governor and to him a petition was sent bearing the required number of signatures (all fictitious save two or three) presented by one Walter H. Brown. The governor appointed three commissioners, Brown, Hoyt and Stillwell. The latter refused to go along with them and these two appointed a Mr. Niese. They named their county seat Brownsdale and located it on Brown's homestead near Andes Creek, an isolated spot in western Douglas County. The county was then bonded for some $40,000 or $50,000. A great deal of secrecy veiled their actions. People became suspicious and the fraud was discovered. Brown and his son were indicted by a Federal grand jury but they disappeared and were not heard of more. In later years, I believe Douglas County had to pay that old debt.

The summer passed pleasantly enough. A bit of ground was broken for the next year's garden, hay put up for the coming winter and a stone and pole shed erected. Our main responsibility was to keep the cattle from straying.

In October, we had an experience, the memory of which will end only with our lives. On a calm blue October day, two of us were tending cattle and playing in a lake bed about a mile from home. All of a sudden we heard a crackling sound and looking up we discovered that the prairie was on fire. We hastily started the cattle for home and were none too soon. By the time we reached the creek a brisk wind had sprung up. We released some penned up calves and drove all to safety on the opposite side of the creek. A little piece of ground had been broken and onto this we piled everything in the house save the cook stove. The fire swept on with unbelievable rapidity and fury, fed by the tall bottom land grass.

Our hay supply was in ashes, our upland grazing ground black as night. There are few more disheartening sights than miles of fire-swept prairie. What a sight to come home to next day. Father and brother had gone to Cedar Island for poles the day before and this sight was what met their gaze on their return. What a prospect for winter! John Baird, grandfather of Merton B. Tice had hay to sell which enabled us to get feed for the winter. $2.50 per ton was the purchase price. The winter of 1881 and 1882 was a very mild one. We had about two weeks of rough weather which was very fortunate for those three families who chose to stay through the winter. Food enough for winter was stored and enough coarse grass for fuel. We whiled away the long winter days and evenings conning over the few school books we brought with us, making guessing games from them, playing jackstones, reciting poems, in fact whatever we could think out.

In February, 1882, to us a very important event occurred. A new neighbor had filed on land and settled just one mile north of us. The family consisted of ten members, all eligible to file on land save three. By 1883 settlers had come in so thick and fast that a bonafide county organization was on and a county seat contest along with it. Three miles east of where Armour now stands, C. E. Huston held a post office and stage route out of Scotland was established. Three miles farther up an Elk Point attorney E. W. Miller had established Douglas City with a route out of Scotland also. The late Jeff Manback was the carrier. Still farther northwest a trio from Mitchell, Prescott Devy and Foster fathered the village of Grandview and won a mail route out of Mitchell. The fight was on. The Grandview sponsors went at the game in a big way. By the time the contest was in full swing, the little village had two newspapers: *Douglas County Chronicle*, George W. Mathews, Editor, and *The Grandview Enterprise*, Woolman Bros., Editors; two general stores; a milliner shop; blacksmith shop; hotel; livery barn and much more. (I think the world was moving as fast then as now.) These Mitchell men were live wires and won easily. Grandview became and remained the county seat for a number of years after the advent of the railroad.

The first Fourth of July celebration ever held in Douglas County was indeed a colorful affair. Many ex-service men of the Civil War period had come to the wilderness to mend their broken fortunes. Among them a fifer named Hosselton. He had several sons who could really play the bugle and drums. About 10 a.m. on the morning of the Fourth, we heard them coming over the hills in their lumber wagon playing the national airs in a way that made the echoes resound. We thrilled, wide-eyed to the first strains of martial music (or any other) that we had ever heard. We hurried to get started for the wonders of a celebration.

The Yankton Sioux Indians had been invited for a feast. They had been gathering for several days and the prairie was dotted with white tents. I thought the whole tribe was there. The celebration opened by the singing of national airs. Then followed the Hosselton band, the reading of the Declaration of Independence and an oration by a young lawyer, John T. Matthews, who had come out from New York. He chose for his subject "Ridpath's Hamilton." I've heard many orations since, but none so outstanding as this early day contribution.

The Indian parade followed. Braves in their war paint and bonnets on horse back, nude save for their breech clouts and feather headdresses with their bodies painted in hideous designs which was a little frightening to those who had never seen anything like it before. They rode fast and yelled and whooped as if getting ready for war.

Several steers were butchered and the feast was on. Most of the celebrants brought their lunches, as eating places were limited. Pink lemonade was $.05 a glass. No ice was available and the lemonade was about the same temperature as the hot July day. After the feast, the Indians put on their war dance with their tom-tom music. The Indian women put on what they called a "squaw dance" a sort of shuffling affair making a circle into which they dragged bystanding young men to dance with them much to the merriment of all.

A bowery floor had been constructed, some fiddlers located and an afternoon dance was under way. Never before had I seen people dance and I thought it the most graceful performance I had ever seen. The ladies wore Gretchen dresses with huge sash bows at the back. Bustles and skirts were in vogue then and the bustles elevated the skirts slightly at the back making a dip in front. They were made of lawn, ankle length and very full-skirted and picturesque. I sat and watched them for a while wondering how they could possibly find their way through the mazes of a quadrille or how to know what the prompter's directions meant. Little did I think that a few years later I'd be going through a similar performance. Two nines of ball players were marshaled from among the celebrants. There was no grand stand, no benches, no shade. It was no fun to sit on the grass in the hot sun with no better protection than a parasol or umbrella so naturally there was a limited number of fans.

Another attraction was the horse races. There was no special track, no entrance fee and any nag could enter the races. There was betting to be sure, but it was light. Nobody was too flush with money and nobody knew the other fellow's horse.

We went home before sunset, somewhat reluctantly. We had hoped to stay for the promised fire works but this was deemed unwise and we mustn't think of it. Such was our first public entertainment. We now had something to talk of for weeks to come.

Schools were not established until 1885. True, there were a few who held school in the homes but these were few and not accessible to but few children.

In the autumn of 1885, a number of the settlers met at our home and held what I believe was the first school meeting in Douglas County. It was agreed to hold a three-month term of school in an abandoned claim shanty. There would be 16 pupils to attend: 3 Pease children; two Wohlfords; two Lesters; 4 Meades, one Brown, one Hunt and 3 Scholtens. Mrs. Minerva Hardin was selected as teacher and the magnificent sum of $15 per month was paid for her services. There was only the bare room. Benches were our seats. The teacher provided some sort of little desk for herself. A stout piece of red building paper was our blackboard and our erasers were pieces of old cloth. Each pupil furnished his own books, many of them handed down. There was no such thing as report cards. Pupils were classed according to their ability to read, write, spell and cipher. Such a conglomeration of books: Barnes, Appleton's and Swinton's Readers; Rays, Robinson's and Appleton's Arithmetics; Harvey's and Read and Kelloggs' Grammars; and ONE history, Swinton's. All who could understand and remember it were in the history class. The teacher read from it daily and expected the pupils to relate what had been read the previous day. This brought out class rivalry and concentration. We never got any farther than the Discovery and Exploration Period and the Revolutionary War for the reason that our terms were three months and each succeeding teacher started us out on page one. We had much of it memorized.

In 1887, school districts were established and small four window school houses were built, equipped with desks, blackboards, erasers and in some instances, globes and lamps. The latter for literary or signing school purposes.

The political election of 1884 was a hotly contested one. Factions had sprung up. Grandview was now "The Hill" and West Grandview. There was much strife for office but school superintendent and the postmastership were outstanding. John T. Mathew, the same who had delivered the Fourth of July address won the election and Frank Tobin, a Mitchell man, was appointed postmaster.

The coming of the railroad brought many changes. Coal could now be purchased from $3 to $5 per ton, lumber for better housing, yard goods, millinery, cheaper groceries, etc.

The old horse power type of threshing machine was brought in by some of the settlers but was doomed to early passing by the coming of the steam engine.

Many stories have been written or related about the blizzard of 1888 but the whole story will never be told. Too many lips are forever closed that might have disclosed varied experiences. All agree that in fury and extent there has never been another that equaled it in the history of the Weather Bureau. The winter of 1949 was worse for heavy snow and duration but covered a smaller area. The "Big Blizzard" swept from Alaska to the Gulf with greater or less violence. The undeveloped Plains states were the hardest hit. No sign or omen preceded that fearful blast. It struck as much as the dust storms of the early 1930s did.

Our family was pretty well scattered that day. We, the younger ones went to school as usual. The storm hit us about 9:30 a.m. My seat was near a window. I could see a hay rake standing about two rods from the building. By 10 a.m., I couldn't see that hay rake. By 10:30 it was raging, hurling great chunks of crusted snow high into the air and falling again in fragments. Our teacher, Charles Palmer, a young man of twenty-two, with the help of five other older boys, wrapped up, joined hands and made their way to the coal house. It took them quite some time to bring in a good supply of coal but at length the job was done. Panting and shaking the snow from their clothing, they dropped down in seats until breath was restored. No more studies for that day. It was too dark and too exciting for further school work. Every one was thinking of the folks at home. The teacher promptly told us that no one would be permitted to leave the building until the storm had spent its fury. He warned us to eat sparingly of our lunches suggesting that we might be there more than one night. There were twelve of us in all. We knew we were there for a while and proceeded to make the best of it. We sang all the songs we knew, told stories, had a court trial, a mock wedding, played games and before we knew it morning had come.

About 4 p.m. the storm had abated and one of our neighbors had arrived to see if we have been sensible enough to stay in the school. He brought sandwiches and coffee to brace us up for the two mile walk home.

What of the folks at home? Father had turned all the stock out and had gone not more than a half mile away for a load of hay accompanied by the hired man. He had the load half on when the storm struck. He started for home but the horses couldn't pull against it. Quickly unhitching he tried to lead them but that failed too. Now he knew he must go with the storm. Presently he found himself in a cornfield. There were three rows of stalks out and three rows standing, thus he knew whose field it was and where he was. He followed it to where a row of trees was standing. He knew he was not far from the home of Joseph Lester. Not daring to leave the trees, he shouted for help. His shout was answered by a shrill whistle. He followed the whistle and managed to get into shelter at last. It was 9 a.m. when he went for the hay and 4 p.m. when he reached Mr. Lester's home. He had saved himself, his hired man and his horses. What of his children? There was no sleep or rest for him the long night through. Early in the morning he started for home not knowing whether he had any children or not.

He found that one of the girls had put in all the stock when the storm struck but couldn't get back to the house and was forced to spend the night in the granary. She kept from freezing by swathing herself in grain bags and fighting off sleep. The other girl kept a light in the window and pounded constantly on tin pans hoping to help someone find the house by means of the noise. Just as my father was about to start in search of the school children the three of us bounced in at the doorway all happy to know that none had perished.

We milked some thirty cows. A Vermont woman, a Mrs. Anderson, was employed to teach us the art of cheddar cheese making. We had a seven screw press, large steam heated vat, hooks of all sizes, draining boards, cheese knives, strainer, drying room and all necessary equipment that goes with the cheese making. We sold from 5 to 25 lbs. of cheese to surrounding towns at $.10 a pound. We pursued this line of endeavor for four years.

I had always cherished a desire to teach school. There were no high schools or institutions of higher learning in this newly settled country. Fifteen months of school was what I had to face the test and could I succeed in writing the teachers' examination.

There was a teachers' institute conducted at Armour offering two weeks of academic work. I screwed up courage enough to write the test. Imagine my joy when a good second grade certificate was the outcome. The County Superintendent sent me to a school of 39 pupils. The school house had seating capacity for only so many. I had to crowd three into one seat. Text books were the private property of the pupils. There were no report cards, course of study or library books. Not even a good blackboard. An improvement had been made in the length of terms. My first school was a six-month term at $30 per month. Board and room $8 per month. I thought my fortune was made and in the bag. This was in November, 1891.

Two things that helped me most in the teaching profession were the teachers' institute in which academic work was done and the state teachers' reading circle. One cultural book, one professional and one historical or literary book was adopted each year by the State Board. The "Schoolmaster in Comedy and Satire," "Lights of Two Centuries," "History of England," "History of France," "White's School Management" were the type of books selected yearly by the state.

After teaching for 36 months in Douglas and Charles Mix Counties, the democrats of Charles Mix County in 1898 elected me to the office of County Superintendent. This I held for four years. In 1905, I was nominated by the Democrats for Superintendent of Public Instruction. The late Dr. George W. Nash was my opponent. The democratic ticket was defeated by 25,000 votes. However I've always been ever grateful for that much recognition, when women couldn't even vote and were of little help to a ticket.

Charles Mix County is large, with more than 150 miles of river front – the Missouri. Up to 1896, it was half the size of its present area. The Yankton Sioux Indian Reservation was opened for settlement, but its development was very slow. Clem Nichols, my predecessor, had organized several township school districts. There was still much more to be done along that line and required much driving on trails with long distances to cover, so I provided myself with a team of ponies and top buggy.

When traveling I put up for lodging wherever night overtook me. After one round of school visitations, I had my stopping places well established. The County Seat was at Wheeler. The court house there was not large enough to supply one room for each officer, so we had to share them. After Geddes was on the map, I did most of my office work there. A typewriter for the County Auditor and one for the County Treasurer were all the County supplied.

It wasn't until 1916 that the County Seat was moved to Lake Andes after several hotly contested elections.

Geddes was centrally located and had set apart a plot of ground and beautified it with trees and shrubs. Platte, Geddes, Lake Andes and Wagner were all in the run for the County Seat honors. Lake Andes wasn't long in getting a Court House that compares favorably with any in the State.

In the summer of 1889, we had the opportunity of listening to an appealing address by Susan B. Anthony on the subject of Woman Suffrage. Four territories were seeking statehood and Miss Anthony hoped the enfranchisement of women would be embodied in the new constitutions. She did a tremendous amount of work traveling by rail or livery team and covering an immense amount of territory making daily speeches fearlessly and capably. I only regret that I did not preserve the unkind comments that local newspapers published.

Miss Anthony succeeded in putting over a portion of her program. Her greatest success was in Wyoming. Women of today may not realize how much they owe to the memory of Susan B. Anthony.

The first great grief of my life overtook me in September, 1898. The Spanish-American war was on and our only brother who was attending college at Wayne, Nebraska, felt it his duty to volunteer for service. He joined the Third Nebraska regiment headed by William Jennings Bryan. They mobilized at Wakefield, training at Ft. Omaha and proceeded to Camp Duba Libre, Florida, in the August heat. Army

beef and typhoid fever proved his undoing and he died there
September 1, 1898, at the age of 26. I have always considered the Spanish-American war as poorly managed and
a blot on our history.

In 1906 I filed on land in Stanley County and was married
there in 1909. Our home life there was brief as my husband
died in 1912. I continued to teach school and raise my one
daughter. In June, 1921, my father was called by death.
A few months later I bought an acreage at Geddes and
moved there in 1923 for the purpose of giving my daughter
educational advantages. The rest of my story is a common
one. I taught school 52 years and doubtless would be doing
so yet had not a paralytic stroke called a halt.

I am fully aware of the hazards and hardships of pioneer
life. I've experienced blizzards, drought, prairie fires, disastrous
hail storms, good times and bad but none the worse for it.

# "My Life and Experiences as a Pioneer Woman"
## Laura Belle Hegarty Schulze
## Gregory County
## 1905

*[Laura Belle Hegarty was born in Clarence, Iowa in 1874 to English-Irish parents. One of the group who organized the Burke Methodist Church, she was Cradle Roll Superintendent for thirty-one years.]*

"Homesteads available in South Dakota" were the words that traveled across the nation in the very first months of 1904. Those were the words that reached us at our home in Hubbard, Iowa, where my husband published the newspaper, and operated a printing shop. The words were of particular interest to us, for, because of the confining nature and the materials used in my husband's work, he had developed lead poisoning, and it was urgently necessary that a change be made in his occupation. So, the opportunity to pioneer on a Homestead in South Dakota, seemed very attractive.

Mr. Schulze and some friends went to South Dakota almost immediately to see the various areas that were being offered. After reviewing a number of them, he filed our claim and our Homestead was located two and one-half miles northeast of Burke, South Dakota.

December passed quickly by, and 1904 yielded to 1905, the momentous year that we would start living on our claim in South Dakota. After all the "good-byes" had been said, the good wishes of friends extended, and the good natured warnings issued, little Harley and I boarded the train and left Hubbard, Iowa, on January 29, 1905, starting our trip to South Dakota. At that time the railroad ended at Bonesteel, South Dakota, and from there on we would travel over the trails to Burke by stage coach.

As the train huffed and puffed across Iowa, little Harley would nap occasionally, and I rode with mingled feelings.

129

Sometimes regret over leaving our friends, off-set by the joy of being with my husband again, then thoughts of the thrills of making our home in a new place, new friends, of the adventures and good times to come, and above all, the thought that the open air would bring good health again.

Thoughts would continue. The difficulties and hardships that beset the Pioneer Woman came to mind, — things that I had read about, and possible crop failures. What about the other people? Supposing that they were not friendly — and the Indians I had heard about, what about them? With those thoughts, admittedly, I was "scared to death," so as the train still puffed along, I thought (at least tried to), only of the good things that were to happen.

Later, after much "puffing" on the part of the locomotive, many, many, "clickety-clacks" as the wheels met the steel rails, we arrived at Bonesteel, South Dakota — the end of the railroad. There we were greeted by a "sample hardship" in the form of a bad blizzard, in fact, so bad that our train was the last one through for several days.

For three days we were snow-bound in Bonesteel only about 25 miles from Burke, our Homestead and my husband. The stage coach made its daily trips, always loaded with people who had been waiting longer than Harley and I. During the three days we naturally became acquainted with others who were waiting to continue over the trails westward. On the fourth day, a young couple, Mr. and Mrs. John Osnes joined with me, and we hired a man to take us to our claims.

Just a few miles of anticipation and it started snowing again, so that it was impossible for our driver to see the trail. We finally reached a house that we saw in the distance and we were given shelter until the storm subsided. Then we continued on to Herrick and there spent the night. The next morning we hired another driver who took us on to Burke and to our claims.

My husband was greatly relieved when Harley and I finally reached Burke. He had driven into Burke each day to see if we had managed to get through the storm. As for myself, I too, was greatly relieved and had successfully passed through one of the hardships meted out to the "Pioneer Woman."

Our sod house was the first I had ever seen, and it really looked good to me after all we had endured throughout the storm. Our Soddy was well built, the roof was of lumber covered with tar paper then a layer of sod, making it leak proof. The walls were plastered, and we had a board ceiling and floor. The floor was covered with linoleum. We had two deep windows, and the side window frames were the only places we could hang our mirrors and other articles. Our Soddy was heated by a coal stove and I used a kerosene stove for cooking—just enough furniture to be comfortable and meet our needs. We found the Soddy to be naturally warm, so it was easy to heat in the winter because of its construction, and was quite cool in the summer. A double wall connected our barn to the Soddy, which my husband felt was necessary because there was danger of having the livestock stolen if one was not close by to watch it.

We always kept a long rope and a shovel in the Soddy. When we had a bad blizzard we would attach the rope to the door and carry it to wherever we were going, so we could find our way back.

One evening when we retired there was a blizzard raging, by morning the snow was up to the roof of our Soddy. My husband opened the door and the snow fell in, it took a lot of hard shoveling and pushing the snow to free ourselves, and to get the snow out of the Soddy.

All of our neighbors had been able to take advantage of the three months extension of time to be on their claims so we were all alone until spring. No telephones and the nearest Doctor was at Bonesteel, South Dakota.

When our neighbors returned to their claims, we tried to meet each Saturday night to visit, play and sing. There was an intense spirit of friendly cooperation, when hard times came along, when a baby was born, and through sickness and death. Friendships were formed that have lasted through our lives.

Our two Indian friends whom I shall always remember were the Red Leafs and the Fool Hawks—both had very nice families. Red Leaf was a minister and one of the hymns he loved to sing for us was "Nearer My God To Thee." Their visits were sometimes a little frightening, because they did not believe in knocking — just open the door and walk in, and make themselves at home.

The prairie fires were frightening, both winter and summer. In the winter the under brush that was not covered with snow would burn, and sometimes it would seem too close for comfort, although the fires were miles away. Our worst fire was set by an Indian, who got off his horse and must have thrown a match in the grass. We saw the fire start so we had a chance to get buckets of water to fight it, and save our house from burning.

The coyotes and their weird howling at night was something that at times gave one a lonely feeling, but their daytime habits were very exasperating. They were the worst chicken thieves we had, and on one occasion a coyote was brave enough to grab a chicken near a cow while my husband was milking. John was so disgusted, he threw the milk.

Rattlesnakes were another hazard. During our first year on the claim my husband killed twenty-seven. Our garden was a short distance from the house, but I never walked through the tall grass, it was safer to ride the pony.

Naturally the lives of the people who go into the unsettled parts of the country as Pioneers, involve much work, hardships, hazards and many times danger. The incidents I have related are typical of the hazards, etc., that one encountered. At the same time the pioneer days spent on our claim had many happy moments and amusing incidents that provided something to talk about, something to laugh about for many years to come.

My husband, John, was a great lover of trees, and admittedly at first he did miss the large trees that were so abundant in his home community. I remember one day he came in and announced that he had found a species of an evergreen tree, it was small so he had placed a piece of fencing around it as a guard. Each day the tree was carefully watered, carrying the water some distance.

One day the folks from a neighboring claim came over to see "John's tree," and somewhat gleefully announced that he was nursing a Russian Thistle along, or it may have been a Tumbleweed, I am not certain which it was. My husband's feelings? Just another "pioneer frustration" which he told about many times in the years to come, and I actually believe that he enjoyed telling it as much as others did listening.

Another incident occurred one Sunday while we were attending Sunday School. On returning home, we found our goat in our Soddy. He had seen his reflection in the mirror at the side of the window, had butted his way through the window, and had fallen into the Soddy. He must have been just as surprised to be in the Soddy as we were to find him there, for he had done very little damage, and was more than anxious to get back into the yard.

There were many wild roses and sweet peas blooming, which added real beauty to the prairie, and made another hobby possible. I gathered rose petals and made them into very fragrant beads for necklaces. Mrs. Emory, an Indian lady, taught me how to do bead work. This was a very interesting hobby.

There were many happy days on the claim, and in later years the children never tired of hearing about "Daddy's Tree" and the many other incidents that occurred while we were pioneering our claim.

Everyone knows that a pioneer is academically defined as "One who goes ahead of other people." With that definition in mind, there is never an end or a limit for the person who has the "Spirit of the Pioneer." There are motives for pioneering: a better life, a better place to live that life, service to the church, the school and the community, and sometimes personal gain. One only needs to look around, and there will be found ample opportunity for either woman or man to be a Pioneer.

# "Meet Stanley County's Oldest Citizen Now 95 Years of Age Residing Near Hayes" Barbara Stump Simmermaker Stanley County 1910

from the *Hayes Booster,* 15 September 1930

*[Although not a "true" Pioneer Daughter, having come to Stanley County (which was organized in 1873) in 1910, Barbara Stump was born in 1835 in Ohio. The youngest in a family of ten, she was two years old when her mother died. When still a child the family moved to Illinois.]*

As the older brother and sisters married, this little girl was kept busy going from one home to another to help out when a new baby arrived or during a busy season and thus missed the chances of learning to either read or write, compulsory education being unheard of at that day and age.

When not helping the family she worked for some of the neighbors and drew the munificent salary of fifty cents a week! The work consisted of milking from two to six or seven cows twice a day, washing dishes and assisting with the cooking and baking and sewing and other household duties and scrubbing the floors after the family had retired and was out of the way. There came a time when she had saved the sum of $5.00 and the immensity of her riches frightened her. Grandma now laughs as she relates that part of the story but she assured me that it was a real problem then. She finally solved it by giving half of it to an older sister who had several small children and buying herself a "few" things.

She had one Sunday dress which was of calico and one pair of shoes and stockings then. When the girls went to church, as they did every Sunday, they walked and carried their shoes and stockings under their arm until they were quite near the meeting place then they slipped out to the side of the road when no one was in sight and put them on. Shoes in those days were far too precious to be worn out unnecessarily.

Of course, children played some, too, even then. Grandma says she used to play house. There were house plants in the homes too. One of the choice varieties being one of dark foliage with beautiful red fruit on it. This fruit was called "love apples" and was given to the children to use in their playhouses with the strict order not to put it in their mouths as it was very, very "poisonous." Today we call these "love apples," tomatoes, and pay as high as fifteen cents per pound for them to eat.

When this little girl of whom you read was about twelve or fifteen years old there was a rumor that a railroad was being built in Illinois and it was quite near to their home. She and her sister walked three miles and from a safe distance peered out from behind some sheltering rocks and bushes and watched some men laying the rails for this new railroad. The workmen were Irish laborers and wore bright red shirts and were considered by these girls little short of barbarians. Those were the good old days when our history tells us the people were afraid that "the locomotive would spoil their farms by its soot and ignite barns and dwellings by its sparks. Its noise would frighten the animals so the hens wouldn't lay and the cows would refuse to give milk."

Although her memory now is failing, she remembers distinctly the time she heard Lincoln and Douglas debate. This was no doubt one of the series of debates held in 1858 or '59, when slavery was the main issue. She says she remembers just how they looked—Douglas so small and dark with such snappy black eyes and Lincoln so tall and slow and gentle-like but not homely, she didn't think. Anyway, Douglas in his speech made a remark to the effect that if Lincoln thought so much of the negro he supposed Abe would like to have one for a wife. When Lincoln got up to answer he slowly replied, "No, I do not want a negro for my wife, neither do I want one for my slave."

Barbara Stump was married to Adam Simmermaker when she was twenty-three. The first of her eleven children were twin boys both of whom are still living. There was no doctor present to usher these wee mites into the world and as the

only one there during those first days who could act as a
nurse was a young niece who was doing the housework, the
young mother was afraid to trust her babies to one so inexperienced so she herself each day bathed and dressed one,
fed it, then laid it at the foot of the bed. Then after she
had rested awhile she took the other boy and bathed, dressed
and fed it also. Those twins are now 67 years young. But
the mother in telling this said, "One baby is a heap of trouble but two is more. After the twins were born I thought
that was trouble enough but there were nine more, only they
came one at a time after that. I never had a doctor for
any of them."

Besides her own brood of eleven she took four grandchildren to raise when the mother died, also two other little
tots whose mother passed away. Later when one of the grandchildren died she had only $5.00 in money and that wasn't
nearly enough to pay for the little coffin. She had a few
geese so she sold them to raise the amount needed for the
burial.

I asked, "Did you spin?" She answered, "Oh yes, of course.
I had to spin and weave and knit for all my children, and
sew all their clothes by hand." A few days ago I picked
up a magazine which contained a full page picture of our
foremost aviatrix and noticed the interviewer, for lack of
something to say, had asked the same question, "Do you
spin?" The answer of today's lady was, "Sure! Tail spin at
an altitude of 3000 feet." Which goes to show the change
during the span of one lifetime.

When Mrs. Simmermaker was 47 years old she still had
five children under school age to care for and two bachelor
brother's-in-law to cook for besides the regular household
duties.

Late in life the family acquired a second-hand sewing
machine to lighten the mother's work but she sewed by hand
for so many years that she never made much use of it. She
still to this day patches the overalls for some of the sons
and grandsons, taking such fine stitches it would put most
of us to shame. She uses glasses only for fine sewing.

Mr. Simmermaker died about twenty-five years ago. Five
years after his death or in 1910 she "came west" with her
sons who took land where they now reside. There are eleven

great grandchildren in the family. Only four years ago she was keeping house for her youngest son and on one occasion when a fine turkey broke its leg accidentally, she quickly dressed it and prepared a delicious turkey dinner with dressing, gravy and all the trimmings and had several guests for dinner.

And as we sat beside her at dinner on this Sunday recently and marveled as she ate with such enjoyment of the delicious spring fried chicken and salad and pickles and vegetables then later of the gooseberry pie and cake and sauce and coffee. I wondered if this could be the wonderful effects of our South Dakota climate or a natural vitality which might withstand any climate.

After dinner she walked out into the yard to have her picture taken for the *Booster*. Later as we were all taking and telling stories she told of an Irishman she had known years ago, who, when he heard of feather beds took one feather and slept on it all night. The next morning he said he had never slept on such a hard bed in his whole life. He said, "Goodness me what would ten pounds be like!" Grandma laughed and said, "Weren't people green then?" I wonder.

                                                        —W.A.Z.

# Katie M. Artz Simon
## Potter County
### 1893

I, Katie M. Artz was born in Mehr, Germany on December 19, 1892 of a German mother and a Dutch father. My parents and I, along with my three older sisters, lived with my maternal grandmother while my father worked in the village. My father's brother, Theodore Artz, a single man, along with several other young men migrated to the United States. My uncle's letters told of the advantages in this new country. He said it was a good place to raise girls (there was no room for more girls in Germany, they said) and encouraged his brother to bring his family to America. So, when I arrived (another girl) my father decided to take his family to America also. In May of 1893 when I was five months old, my father, mother, and three sisters: Anna, Tina and Mary and myself sailed for New York.

My mother was so seasick that she was in bed most of the trip, while we girls played around in her room. What an awful trip it must have been for mother. We were held up on Ellis Island for several days because my oldest sister, Anna, was crippled. We were locked in an old hotel room. All we had to sleep on was a wire spring with no blankets. No matter how hard we pounded on the door no one opened it. Finally the doctor came to examine my sister. There were no xrays to determine what was wrong but they finally passed her and we were allowed to proceed by train to South Dakota. Later we found out that my sister was born without hip sockets, so was lame all her life, but she made a good active life for herself.

During the summer of 1893 the train brought us to Bowdle, South Dakota where John Arntz, a friend, was supposed to meet us. But being we were several days late, he had given up waiting for us and had gone home, so we all slept in the depot on the floor. The next day our friend returned for us with food and took us first to his home and then to a parcel of land with a one room house and an attached shed. The shed contained cow chips which my uncle had gathered for fuel but it had rained and soaked the chips so there was nothing to burn. The next day my mother wanted to cook a ham bone which they had brought along but there was no fuel. So one of the men took an old saw and cut down the only tree in the area to make a fire to cook the food. My mother cried and said they should have stayed in Germany.

My father finally bought a team of horses and he homesteaded eight miles west of Hoven, South Dakota in Potter County. The first house was built partly under ground with a roof over the top. This house had two rooms, one was the bedroom for the children, the other was the living room and kitchen and also a sleeping room for my parents. Later a small house was moved along side and used as a kitchen.

I went to a public school one mile from my home. Mrs. Raymond Robinson, a farmer's wife, was my first teacher. She held the classes in her home for a few months until the school was built. I was the youngest pupil and I remember when I got tired in school, the teacher would let me lie on the floor with a pillow and rest.

As we children got older we would have to help with the work at home so went to school only in the winter time. We helped pick corn in the fall. My oldest sister, Anna, was crippled, so she was sent to school, graduating from the eighth grade with the highest average in the county. Then she went to business college in Aberdeen. My sister, Tina, helped dad in the fields and after finishing school she left to become a nun. My mother developed rheumatism, so they called it then, now we would call it arthritis. She was very sick and became very crippled. My sister Mary and I changed off going to school and staying home to do the house work and take care of mother. When Mary finished the eighth grade she went to Gettysburg to take a teacher's training course and also sewing lessons. I, being the oldest left at home, quit school during my last year to care for the house.

The babies were all born at home with the help of a midwife, Mrs. Erickson. I remember coming home from school and finding my mother in bed, crying and holding the dead baby, one week old. It was the first of our family laid to rest in our new country.

I remember the heating in our basement house. We had a straw burner. This had two drums which were packed with straw. One lasted about all night. This was used for heating and cooking. After we had the new house we had a hard coal burner for heat and we used cow chips in the cooking range in the summer time.

We had a spring wagon and a team. Later this was replaced by a buggy. We got our mail at Pembroke where Mrs. Emil Udahl had the post office in her home.

The neighbors often helped each other with work. Then there would be get-togethers of adults and children, when they would visit, eat, drink beer, and sing German songs.

I remember coming home from school one Christmas and telling my mother that the other children were hanging up their stockings and that a man called Santa Claus would fill them. So we hung our stocking before going to bed. How poor mother hunted for raisins, and what else she could find in the cupboard to put in those stockings.

I became a teenager and our social life developed into socials and dances usually held by the church organizations. The Catholic Church was the center of life in Hoven, our closest town. It was at these functions where I met the Simon brothers. They lived on a farm about four miles south of Hoven. They had nice buggies and horses and they were good dancers. My parents let me go to dances once a month if one of my older sisters went along. Leo started courting me. He was born in Potter County on October 17, 1886. He would come and get me with a buggy and team for dances, house parties or for dinners at his relatives.

We were married on June 8, 1911 in the old Hoven church by Father A. C. Helmbrecht. My wedding dress was ordered from National Bellas Hess but my father made the check out to Sears Roebuck by mistake as that is where most of the orders usually came from. So my dress did not arrive and we had to make a hurried trip by buggy to Gettysburg to get material and my sister Mary made my dress. Our wedding day was very hot and dry. The dinner was held at the Simon place because they had a bigger house and also my mother was sick and not able to do the work. My father-in-law, Stephen Simon was a county commissioner, and was well known in the community, so he wanted to invite everyone. So there was a big crowd at our wedding. We drove to church in a hired car and also to a free wedding dance in the evening.

We moved on to a farm six miles west of Hoven on the West Half of Section 3, 120-75. We had no crop that first summer because of the drought but we managed to get along. We picked cow chips and cut wood for fuel. We had a few cows to milk and some pigs and five horses. With a little help from our good parents, we put in another crop in the spring of 1912.

That spring I was expecting our first child. One day I felt that I was about to go into labor and Leo was out in the field walking behind the drag. I was to turn on the windmill if I needed help. He came in and took the team and buggy and went to get his mother, Christina Simon who acted as midwife for relatives, friends, and neighbors. That night April 16, 1912 our first son, Henry, was born.

It was another hot, dry summer and not much crop but we did get a little hay for cattle feed.

On May 10, 1913 our first girl, Laura, was born. Then we each had one to rock in the two rocking chairs that we got for wedding gifts.

That summer we again did not have much of a crop, so Leo and his brother Ed and brother-in-law, Pete Schaefer took horses, wagons and header boxes and drove to North Dakota to work in the harvest fields as crops were good there. They earned good wages. My sister, Mary, who taught school near by, stayed with me nights and I did the chores on the farm. One day I was churning butter with a barrel churn with little Henry on my lap. We would sing "Come butter come," and then "Come Daddy Come" when we heard some one drive up and there was daddy. But little Henry was afraid of daddy since he had been gone about a month and he had let his whiskers grow during that time. Baby Laura was too small to be afraid.

We did get good crops the next few years and bought a tractor and also bought the land we lived on in 1916. We raised more cattle and hogs and hired help and life became easier.

[When the children were ready for school, the family moved to Hoven, where Leo became the John Deere agent, and Katie "took care of the machine shop as parts-man and bookkeeper." They sold the first combine in Potter County. "Believe me, we were busy," Katie said, as they were still farming on the side. As time went on, their sons helped them operate a filling station and Livestock Sales Ring. In old age, Katie and Leo traveled and enjoyed their fifty-two great grandchildren. Katie Simon died at the Holy Infant Hospital, Hoven, South Dakota at the age of eighty-one.]

# Martha Habersdotter Johnson Tisdall
## Walworth County
## 1886

*[Born in Bergan, Norway in 1833, one of a large family of brothers and sisters, Martha Habersdotter early in life developed the aptitude for the care of the sick that was to carry her from her native Norway, first to Wisconsin, then Iowa, and eventually to Dakota Territory.]*

Trained in the old and honorable Scandinavian profession of midwifery, she fulfilled the tradition of generations of the women in her family. With a little black satchel, the hallmark of her profession as midwife, and still a young girl, she came to Wisconsin just prior to the Civil War.

Then she married a Mr. Johnson, of which union a child, Oliver, was born. Her husband, a soldier in the Civil War, was killed early during the first year of that war.

Joining relatives in Cass County, Iowa, she met and married Johannes Tisdall, a widower with six children. She came with him to Blue Blanket Territory in 1886.

Her fame as a trained midwife spread from her own community to those adjoining. She was many years ahead of her generation in the firm conviction that cleanliness is the first requisite in the care of illness.

Martha Tisdall went about combating age-old superstitions and the sour disapproval of the medical profession. She substituted clean hot water for warm chicken blood or weasel skins for treatment of infections, and boiled water and boiled milk in typhoid cases, clean linen and rigid sanitation for obstetrics. The physicians of her day gave her, first grudging acceptance, and finally whole-hearted admiration and respect.

Mrs. Tisdall delivered many babies all alone, often under the most trying circumstances. No one ever asked her help in vain.

She had a congenitally crippled hip, which was a handicap to her. Nevertheless, she carried on.

One time, during the breaking of the ice on the Missouri River, Mrs. Tisdall crossed the river in a row boat to get to her patient. One big Indian rowed the boat, another fended off the swirling chunks of ice that threatened to smash the boat, but she was needed on that other side and she went.

In later years she became Grandma Tisdall, not alone to her own grandchildren, who are numerous, but to the whole community.

She was mother to thirteen children. She died in 1914 at the age of 81.

# Viola Elizabeth Sherman Trumble
## Sully County
## 1885

by her daughter, Delta Elisabeth Trumble-Fiedler

Viola Elizabeth Sherman was born in Prince George, Virginia, December 29th, 1861, too near Christmas to ever get any birthday presents or have much of a celebration on her birthday anniversary. She was the fourth child of Charles Jiles Sherman and his wife Mercey Maria Conley-Sherman. Her birth place was the plantation owned and operated by George Dan'ls, — that's the way they said it, Dan'ls, — where her father worked as overseer of the negro slaves, called a slave-driver in the language of the time and place. There she spent her early childhood, the first four years of her life. Playing with the negro children she learned their ways and language, and the southern drawl learned then stayed by her unto her later years.

In 1865 the danger of civil war between the slave holding states and the non-slavery states was too close for comfort, and the Shermans literally fled back to New York state, their former home.

In New York her father worked as a stone mason, and died of Mason's consumption when Viola was ten years old. She remembered him as a kind father. She and her older sister were frequently called early in the morning to get breakfast so that mother Mercy could rest longer in bed. He was several years older than his wife and took much of the burden of managing the family household.

Mother Mercy was however plenty busy. She did all the sewing for the family. She first made the cloth of flax or wool or cotton then cut her own patterns and made the entire wardrobe for the family. Viola learned to sew as she helped with these chores. She was a grown girl before she had a "boughten dress" as the ready-made dresses sold at the stores were called. Perhaps the family disliked the home spun, home-made garments, but they wore well, and the carding, weaving and spinning learned then was proudly recalled in the latter years on the South Dakota Prairie. The sewing learned there was an invaluable asset all through her life.

After the death of Charles Jiles Sherman, his wife had six young mouths to feed. So it was necessary for her to allow as many as were able to go out to work for board and what wages they could command. Viola worked several summers in the tanning factory and in the logging camps and lumber mills. Her wage besides board was $1 per week. She received little regular schooling, sometimes was able to get as much as three months in a year if her employer was willing and helpful. As she grew older she worked as hired girl and made more headway, both educationally and financially. Her most loved employer was Mrs. Joe Ferris, who was always spoken of as a good friend.

When she was 22 she married a young man of the community whose 27 years of life had been a good deal like her own. They met at a harvesters dinner where Viola helped serve. Milo was so enamored by her beauty and grace that he almost forgot to eat, so that when she came by to refill the coffee cups his was still untouched. Realizing this as she started to pass him by he grabbed his cup and said "Wait A-Minute" and gulped the coffee so she had to fill his cup also. That incident brought him to her attention. She was slender, blue-eyed with brown hair, rosy cheeked and pugged nosed. He was dark, tall and handsome with shoulders slightly stooped because he had been doing a man's work every since he was twelve years old.

Their courtship was a proper and prudent affair. He called regularly every two weeks on Sunday, – tho at first he used the alternate Sunday to "Go see" Reta, another girl-friend. Reta soon found out about Viola and "gave him the mitten" in vigorous fashion. And whatever they talked about, it wasn't money or marriage relationships. Viola said in later life that if she had known that he believed that the man of the family should keep and manage all the family money she would not have married him, for though he always gave the money she asked for if he had it, she always resented having to ask him for money.

On November 7th, 1883 Viola Elizabeth Sherman became Mrs. Milo E. Trumble at Chatham, Pennsylvania. The Rev. E. W. Miller was the marrying pastor and her younger sister, Eleanora and brother George were the signed witnesses. The bride wore a dark wine colored dress of boughten wool cloth of a wide herring-bone weave, — made up in the fashion of the day by her own hand. The skirt was full, with at least 12 gores held out by several flounced petticoats. The fitted waist was held straight by stays around the belt line with a flaring peplum below. The leg-'o mutton sleeves gathered a couple yards of material into the armhole and the deep tight fitting cuff at the elbow. A velvet facing was buttoned down the front from throat to belt with at least two dozen small round gold buttons over which neatly hand made button holes looped. At the throat was a gold bar-pin. The dress served as the "best dress" for special occasions for many years. It was ultimately made over into "best dresses" for her daughters years later. The groom wore conventional black.

The young couple set-up housekeeping on a small farm which allowed room to keep a cow and some chickens. Milo continued work at the mill.

There was much talk of greater opportunities out west. Linus Willie, Milo's only brother, had located out there and kept writing for them to "come to Dakota." And so they made plans. Their first baby was born in April 1885. So it was that in September of that year they sold the cow and chickens, packed everything else they could into two chests and "took the excursion" to Pierre, (Pee-air they called it). The baby, George Chauncey, was six months old on the train. And they had come to the end of the line. It can be truthfully said that they stayed because they did not have passage back whence they came.

Will met them at the station with a team and wagon and took them out to this home where they were welcomed by his wife Elizabeth and little son Edwin. They staid with Will and Elizabeth several months while the land was filed on near by and the sod house was being built and the trees were being hauled from the Missouri River 15 miles away and set out to make the ten acres of trees for the tree claim. Some of the more hardy of these boxelders still stand in

1950, but the sod house is gone, not even a picture of it remains, except in imagination.

Thus began a new education for Viola, a new life, – the strenuous, lonely, terrifying, good life of the pioneer woman of the plains. She learned to make good meals out of flour and salt pork, for vegetables were scarce after the garden stuff gave out. She kept house neatly in their little 10 by 12 sod shack. There was a wide board floor in the end where the bed set, the rest was dirt floor, dirt made smooth and crusty by damp'ning and sweeping. She learned to make baby clothes out of the flour sacks after she had washed and bleached them white. She bore another son in December 1887, a puny baby, never very well. She thought it was because she hadn't had meat to eat while she "was carrying him." This fear was only partly dispelled when years later the doctor put her daughter-in-law on a meatless diet during pregnancy for the good of both the mother and the baby. He was their first Dakota child.

That winter of 1887-88 was a humdinger. January 12, 1888 made history and a good argument against trying to settle the prairie plains, by lashing snow too fine to see through on waves of cold wind in a blizzard that if we take the word of the old timers who saw it was truly the "granddaddy of them all." During that storm Milo kept a path to the hay-shed they called a barn by making the trips to the hay stack every 1/2 hour to fill the hay burner by which they kept the house warm. Who can say what those days were like to young parents with two small boys, when the nearest neighbor was a mile away over the snow or through the blizzard? They attended to the business at hand, what else could they do? And thus won out with the Dakota Prairie. Thus they built up home and family.

Six children were born, four boys and two girls. Viola's babies were all born at home with the help of a "mid-wife" or a good neighbor woman. She never had much help in the house, money was scarce and hard to get, credit for the newcomers was nil, so the money went to pay for the necessary things out of doors and help with the farm and stock. One baby, a boy, came at seven months and died three days afterward, and her second son, the first Dakota child of the family, died after 27 years of illness and pain, in another winter of deep snow, 1915.

Viola would do anything to "keep the Sunday school going," even when there was no pastor at the church community of Okobojo, S.D. She was superintendent of the Sunday School and kept the Sunday School papers and Golden Text cards coming for all who would attend.

There were pie socials, and basket suppers at the hall to raise money for this and that, or even to pay the preacher. Always every Christmas there was a big tree at the hall at Okobojo and a program befitting the occasion. Aunt Belle Mateer, Mrs. Chas. "saw to it" that there were presents for the children. She was the organist for all occasions, many times playing for the Saturday night dance then after a quick trip home to get breakfast returned to the same organ in the same hall to play for Sunday School and Church. Okobojo grew to be the center of social activities as well as a convenient inland trade center through from it's early beginning as a stopping place in the early '80's to '90's. There were 3 stores, a printing office, a hotel, a slaughter house, a sorghum mill, a town hall and a school besides the residences of the families who ran the businesses. But by the turn of the century people began to move away and now in 1950 there is little left to prove that early activity.

About the time the boys were ready for school Viola and Milo moved into the house on the Okobojo creek, where he had filed on a homestead, built a house and dug a well, to be near the school. Here they spent the winters for several years, and here Viola staid with the girls and one of the boys to care for the stock near the well during the summers while Milo farmed and cut hay on the prairie, until 1907 when the artesian well was drilled on the tree claim place, and a house was provided so they could again live on the prairie place.

The monotony of the pioneer life was relieved on rare occasions by a visit to the neighbors', usually lasting overnight. Hardships were not forgotten but shared. One of the hardships that aggravated Viola was the ever present bed bugs, flies and mosquitoes, to say nothing of the rattlesnakes. Probably every child of that period has a seeming inborn caution about rattlesnakes, and while they were numerous they moved into the house only on rare occasions. But the bed bugs were ever present, and permeated the wood bedsteads of that time until there just wasn't any getting rid of them. Viola kept them down by putting carbolic acid into the cracks of the bedstead with a wing feather from a chicken as applicator. She sat up at night to catch them as they came out of the wall boards. The lumber was full of them, and they came in the mail. Everybody had bedbugs and flies. Covered dishes were used on the table to keep the food away from the flies. There were no screens at the windows and no DDT in those days. Yet with all these difficulties Viola was a marvelous housekeeper. Her washings hung in proper order on the line each washing whiter than the one before, because she used unbleached muslin for bedding and underclothes, and home-made lye soap. Her knowledge of sewing stood her in good stead those days. She made most of the clothes for the family from the bolts of goods she brought home from those perhaps yearly trips to Pierre when she had $25 to $50 with which to buy a years supply.

She was never very well, but she "kept going" as she used to say, and did accomplish a great deal of work in that puttering, particular way she did things. And if the first 50 years of her life were pretty hard to take, it was partly made up to her by the comfort and, dare I say, happiness of the latter years in town with a house that had everything she had ever wanted and a church near by. Viola wasn't a happy seeming person. She often covered her joy by scolding, just as she talked out her fears in nagging, — ever harping on the should-be-forgotten mistake. Thus she seemed to dilute her happiness a little and really did deflate the expected joy in others trying to do something particularly nice for her.

They say that she died, but she didn't really. She lives on in her children and grand children, in the looks and ways that are the same as her looks and way. They seem to be just latter editions with revisions as necessary to bring them up to date. And if each of them does as much better for their children as she did for her family in giving her children a better chance than she had in her younger days, the super-race may not be as far off as some would have you think.

# Sarah Wood Ward
## Yankton County
### 1868

"As I stepped off the stage coach I felt as though I must have some loving, friendly woman's greeting. I felt so alone and there was no one."

At dusk on Nov. 6, 1868 the stage coach from Sioux City brought to Yankton, Dakota Territory, my father, Joseph Ward, and my mother, Sarah Wood Ward, his bride of a few months. The contrast between Sarah Ward's home in Pawtucket, Rhode Island and this new country was enough to daunt the heart of the most courageous of women. Reared in a home of wealth and culture, brought up by sound orthodox New England principals and customs, Sarah Wood Ward was now in an entirely different world.

The ride over the wide expanse of country between Sioux City and Yankton, without a tree except scrubby plumb brush and only occasionally a small house seen in the distance, was the beginning of Sarah Ward's new life as wife of a Home Missionary. By nature she was shy and retiring, fearful of the new and strange experiences that were ahead of her. Sarah Ward's deep religious faith and her devotion to the cause of missions were the strongholds which upheld and guided her in all the early years.

In later life Sarah Ward seldom spoke of these lonely early days but as I recall some of her statements, it is impressed on my mind that the early pioneer women were heroes no less than the men. They kept their fears, sorrows and homesick moments locked in their hearts and carried on without faltering.

Sarah Ward's duties as wife of the new minister began at once. They arrived on November 6th and Joseph Ward preached his first sermon November 8th in the Capitol building behind a pulpit made out of a dry-good box covered with cloth. Prayer meetings were begun also, the first one on the Wednesday following that first Sunday of preaching.

The ladies of Yankton carried on the important tasks of keeping up the social and financial activities of the church. They met at the different homes, crowded into rooms often scantily furnished with dry-goods boxes serving as both chairs and tables. At the end of most of these gatherings supper was served, the men coming in to eat as well, with children running in and out. In speaking of these gatherings, Sarah Ward said it was worth much in developing a true Christian fellowship among the people of Yankton.

These pioneer women, eager for the church privileges they had left behind in the east, worked diligently in raising funds for a church building. Their crowning achievement was a wonderful bazaar at the old St. Charles Hotel which stood on the site of the present Yankton Hotel.

The church was built in a little over a year after Joseph and Sarah Ward arrived in Yankton, and a year or so later, became self-supporting.

The Home Missionary spirit and zeal which Joseph and Sarah Ward brought to Dakota carried their congregation beyond the point of their own self support, so that soon they, in turn, were aiding in the establishment of new churches in Dakota.

It was this missionary zeal and desire to give everyone in Dakota territory a chance for spiritual growth and worship that filled a large part of Sarah Ward's busy life. She carried on (in long hand) a large correspondence as Territorial Secretary of home missions. She used to tell of how often she wrote holding me in her left arm, with my brother Sheldon standing on the back rung of her chair, pulling her ear.

Sarah Ward's life was a full and busy one. Her children were not neglected because of other duties. She kept up the standards of a home such as she came from. She shielded her husband from unnecessary interruptions as he was busy in his study. She entertained guests almost constantly. Hotel accommodations being limited, ministers, missionaries and others stopped at the Ward home. My earliest recollections of meal time were of sitting almost always at a long table with many outside the family group.

As I said before, my mother seldom spoke of the very early days to her children. Possibly we, like many other children, were not so interested in a past, so didn't ask her about it. However, I know that Sarah Ward suffered much in heart and mind in those first years, and to speak of them later in life often made her sad. But this one statement from her I well remember: "No one will ever know how much I feared the Indians during those first years. I would be working in my kitchen and turn around to see one standing behind me or peering in the window. They were not unfriendly, merely curious." But with rumors often about of Indians on the war path coming to wipe out Yankton, Sarah Ward found it hard to believe that the Indians living on the bluffs where Yankton College now stands, and in the plum brush near the Missouri River, had no plans of hostile attack.

Besides the Indians to fear, Yankton had the reputation of being one of the worst river towns — full of lawlessness and wickedness. Bear and whiskey flowed freely, and as a result, there were many fights and shootings. One such event, while not disastrous to life, presents a picture in great contrast to the conventional New England of Sarah Ward's early home. Sarah Ward's youngest brother, Albert Wood, was out here in the early days. He, with Mr. Potter, ran a jewelry store. One day a man entered the store, a man typical of the wild reckless western country. Pointing to a large wall clock he asked, "How much?" My uncle said "$50." The man raised his gun, shot accurately each of the twelve figures on its face, laid down 50 dollars and walked out.

In contrast to those in this new country who had let former standards slip and lived lives lawless and uncurbed, there was in Yankton a group of people whom mother called "the cream of the East." Like Joseph and Sarah Ward, these men and women came from eastern homes of refinement and culture. It is this group, including such names as Edmunds, Beadle, Todd, Faulk, Tripp, Miner, Foster, French, that set the standards of living for our state, and it is to the women of this group that a large share of credit should be given. In spite of terror, fear and home-sickness, they stood by to uphold the hands of their husbands, and, in spite of difficulties, brought up their children by the same high standards and principles which had been their own training in the East.

Imbued so constantly and deeply with the missionary spirit, Sarah and Joseph Ward did not neglect the religious and missionary training of the children. In addition to Sunday School, there was organized a children's missionary Society know as "Willing Hearts." This society met every other Saturday afternoon at the Ward Home. About fifty children came each time. Stories of Missions were told, games played, and some time spent in making articles to be sold on a later date at a missionary Fair. This last activity of the day was directed by Joseph Ward for the boys, in the basement where he had a shop. The girls were in the parlors under Sarah Ward's supervision, sewing and making articles.

To build thus for the children was an early fulfilling of Article I of the modern present day children's charter worked out at President Hoover's White House Conference which reads as follows:

"For every child, spiritual and moral training to help him stand firm under the pressure of life. The mothers of today have to screw their courage to the sticking point in order to put over one real part of fifty for their children." How my mother could stand it through all those years to open her home to fifty children every other Saturday is more than I can understand.

The latter years of my father's life were even fuller for Sarah Ward. He was away a great deal in the interests of Yankton College. His health was breaking which added to her burden in worry. She had almost the full responsibility of guiding her growing children, entertaining guests, and keeping up the ever larger home missionary correspondence. She locked in her heart the increasing belief that her husband's days were numbered, and carried on, upheld by her faith.

After my father died in December, 1889, my mother went east to be with friends and relatives for a time. When she returned, she had to plan for the future of herself and the children. Practically all of the considerable amount of money left Sarah Ward by her father, Joseph Wood of Pawtucket, Rhode Island, had gone into the college. Being used to living on a comfortable scale, it was a hard task to cut down and give up many of these comforts. Sarah Ward did it and taught her family to accept cheerfully this new way of living.

Although she shrank from public appearance, being sensitive and shy by nature, Sarah Ward, because of needed

income and because of her deep interest in Missions, acted
as Home Missionary of the Lesterville Community for two
years. Her active interest in this work resulted in the building
of a church in Lesterville.

My memories of these two years was the joy I had in
going with my mother every Saturday by train to Lesterville, about 30 miles from Yankton. She had a room upstairs
in the Depot provided by my mother's fine and staunch
friends, the Station Master, Mr. Plumb, and his wife. Each
week end was a thrill to me—the train ride up, the sleeping
in a room so near the trains that went by at night, and
the riding back Monday or Tuesday morning in the caboose
at the end of a long freight train. I remember expressing
a wish to mother that we might live always in a house right
next to the railroad tracks. I can still hear her gasp and
say, "Oh no!"

It was many years later before I came to realize how
hard this work was for her: the preparation of the weekly
sermon, the harder task of delivering it, and the leaving
of the other children alone those 2 or 3 days.

Leaving this work, Sarah Ward took active part in raising funds for Yankton College. For several years she spent
the winters in the East, speaking in churches and before
various groups on behalf of Yankton College. Through her
writings and personal contacts she gave unstintingly of herself
for the college that was so dear to her.

These winters away from her children meant a supreme
sacrifice for Sarah Ward. She wanted to be with her family
to love, guide and care for them in the home. Any type
of public appearance was hard for her, but, typical of her
whole life, she never shrank from her duty and never thought
of her own personal desires if they conflicted with the plans
laid out for her as she saw it.

It seems to me that a tribute to the care and training
of her children in the earlier years is shown in the fact that,
during all those winters away from her children, they seemed
to grow, develop and carry on as any normal family group
without any glaring misconduct. As I look back on those
years I feel sure of these things:

1. The good foundation she gave us of wanting to choose the better things.

2. Our deep love for her and our respect for her word.

3. The training and obedience which she gave us.

4. Her faith in us to do the right thing.

Because we respected and obeyed her, we accepted the authority she gave the eldest member of the family, my sister Ethel. We often argued with her, but it never occurred to us to defy her.

Sarah Ward's last years were spent quietly in the old home. Her strenuous life took its toll and the last few years were of semi-invalidism. But she kept up to the last her interest in all the things that had been her life's work and joy—the church missions and Yankton College.

As the years go on, I look back over my mother's life and these impressions stand out clearly: her deep religious faith and the strength and comfort she got each day from her quiet moments of prayer and Bible reading; her patience in dealing with our faults together with her firmness of purpose in guiding us right; the kind of helpful, friendly spirit she showed to the forlorn members of the community who came to see her; the constant devotion to her duty; the courage it took for one as sensitive and retiring as was Sarah Ward by nature to go forth after her husband's death and preach the Gospel, and later, plead for funds for Yankton College.

Of such quality were the pioneer women of South Dakota. They were not in the public eye as were the men, but by their quiet and unselfish devotion to these men of early Dakota, they, as well, should go down in history as builders of our state.